A Time for Peace

Reflections on the meaning
of Peace and Violence in the Bible

Herman Hendrickx

First published in the Philippines in 1986 as *Peace, Anyone?*
by Claretian Publications, Quezon City
This edition first published in Great Britain in 1988
SPCK, Holy Trinity Church, Marylebone Road, London NW1 4DU

British Library Cataloguing in Publication Data

Hendrickx, Herman
  A time for peace.
  1. Bible. Special subjects. Peace.
  I. Title
  220.8'327172

ISBN 0 281 04397 3

Photoset by Inforum Ltd, Portsmouth
Printed in Great Britain by Hazell Watson Viney Limited,
Member of BPCC plc, Aylesbury, Bucks

For everything there is a season,
and a time for every matter under heaven . . .
a time to keep silence, and a time to speak;
a time to love, and a time to hate;
a time for war, and a time for peace.

Ecclesiastes 3.1, 7—8

Contents

Part Two: Violence

Foreword

There is a collection of charming line drawings by the cartoonist Mel Calman entitled *My God*. One of these cartoons shows God looking somewhat disconsolate and saying, 'Oh dear, I think I have lost my copy of the Divine Plan'. Looking at the state of the world one might be forgiven for wondering whether God ever had one. It seems that in his ordering of the world he had arranged things in such a way that life would be made extremely difficult for those who sought to provide credible theodicies, justifications for the ways of God. You would have thought God might have organised things a bit better – that there would have been enough rain for everybody, instead of having devastating floods in Bangladesh and equally devastating droughts in the Sahel.

Even more distressing perhaps are all those instances of man's inhumanity to man – holocausts, repression, injustice, violence, war and rapacity. An atheist or agnostic would probably have a field day: 'Just look at the squalor and repression in Chile, Haiti, in all of Latin America. What about Afghanistan, the Philippines, South Korea, Sri Lanka, Kampuchea? How can you bear the catalogue of violence and suffering in the Lebanon and the war between Iran and Iraq? What about Ulster and Israel and the Palestinians? What about Ethiopia and the horrible atrocities of Renamo in Mozambique and the casualties in Angola and Namibia? What about the legalised institutionalised violence of apartheid, the detention of even children, the mass population removals and the violence of bomb blasts allegedly by those who want to overthrow apartheid?'

The publication of *A Time for Peace: Reflections on the meaning of Peace and Violence in the Bible* could not be more timely. Discussions of violence especially have sadly been characterised by generating more heat than light because those caught up in situations of violence from the nature of the case find it extremely difficult to be dispassionate. The perpetrators of violence and those who benefit willingly or unwillingly from an unjust socio-political and economic dispensation are often afflicted with a myopia that precludes their recognising the violence of the system which maintains the status quo from which they benefit. The victims tend to believe that virtually anything they do against that system could be justified.

It is good to have a scholarly attempt to find out what the Bible actually teaches on these emotive subjects. God be praised that peace is a comprehensive thing – wholeness, integrity, embracing physical and spiritual well-being, prosperity and communal health, and fellowship based on justice. Pope Paul VI said, 'If you want peace, work for justice', and what he said was scriptural through and through. I am glad too that the Bible does not usually castigate the oppressed as being violent – violence being what they suffer at the hands of the powerful and the rich. It is good to hear that really we Christians probably ought to be pacifists, for Jesus taught his followers how to die and not how to kill, that we must never demean and dehumanize the other by turning him into an enemy we can kill.

A Time for Peace makes a new and immensely valuable contribution to the discussion of violence, non-violence, justice and peace and I hope many will take the time to reflect on its insights and let these make a difference to a world crying desperately for peace and justice.

†*Desmond Tutu*
Archbishop of Cape Town

Acknowledgements

Scripture quotations are from the Revised Standard Version of the Bible, copyrighted 1946, 1952, © 1971, 1973 by the Division of Christian Education of the National Council of the Churches of Christ in the USA, and are used by permission.

The extracts from *Theological Dictionary of the New Testament*, G. Kittel and G. Friedrich (eds), vol. II, are reproduced by permission of SCM Press.

The extracts from *Jesus and the Politics of His Day*, E. Bammel and C.F.D. Moule (eds), are reproduced by permission of Cambridge University Press.

The extracts from *The Old Testament and Theology* by G.E. Wright are reproduced by permission of Harper & Row, New York.

The extracts from *Christ and Violence* by R.J. Sider are reproduced by permission of Herald Press, Scottdale, PA.

The extracts from *The Gospel According to Luke X–XXIV* by J.A. Fitzmyer and *Invitation to the New Testament: Epistles* IV by F.W. Danker are reproduced by permission of Doubleday and Co., New York.

The extract from *Jesus Before Christianity* by A. Nolan is reproduced by permission of Darton, Longman & Todd.

The extracts from *Taking Sides* by A. Nolan are reproduced by permission of the Catholic Truth Society.

Part One

Peace

1. Peace in the Old Testament

A. Peace in the Hebrew Bible (shalom)

Not counting a number of proper names, like Jerusalem or Absolom, the word *shalom* and the words derived from it occur more than three hundred and fifty times in the Old Testament. The root meaning of *shalom* (*slm*) is 'to be sound', 'to be safe', and its fundamental idea is totality. Anything that contributes to wholeness can be expressed in terms of *shalom*. The following paragraphs illustrate some of the many facets of *shalom*.

Shalom and community

Shalom forges community, which in turn includes common participation in God's blessings. In the community which enjoys *shalom*, there is *harmony* and *opportunity* for *growth* for all in all respects. With *shalom* like this, *wholeness* and *integrity* are developed in the individual members of the community, and this forges *shalom* in the community as a whole. This wholeness and well-being of the community are endangered by self-centredness and selfish acts.

Shalom as health and prosperity

Shalom's root meaning of wholeness relates it to *health* and *well-being*. So, for instance, Jacob inquires about

Laban. 'Is it well (*shalom*) with him?' and the shepherds reply, 'It is well' (Gen 29.6).

The common greeting of *shalom* involves wishing for the health, the well-being of the person greeted (e.g. Sam 10.4). When people are ill there is no *shalom* in their bones! (Ps 38.3).

The story of Joseph (Gen 37—50) illustrates *shalom* as *prosperity*, while containing some references to *shalom* in human relationships. Joseph's brothers could not speak with *shalom* to Jacob because he favoured Joseph (Gen 37.4). In all Joseph's troubles in Egypt God was with him and brought prosperity to Potiphar's house because of Joseph (Gen 39.5). The troubled Pharaoh received an answer of *shalom* from God through Joseph (Gen 41.16).

Shalom, translated 'prosperity', is paralleled with wealth: 'Behold, I will extend *prosperity* (*shalom*) to her like a river, and the *wealth* of the nations like an over-flowing stream' (Isa 66.12).

Shalom and war

We easily think of peace as the opposite of war, and this idea is not totally absent from the biblical writings. However, the Hebrew Bible does not simply equate peace with the absence of war.

If people live in *shalom*, they enjoy health, wholeness, soundness and integrity. Living harmoniously with one's family adds to *shalom*. The wider the 'covenant' of peace extends, the more inclusive is *shalom* (eg, Gen 26.28–31; 28.21; 34.21, 30).

Sometimes seeking peace resulted in becoming vassals of Israel rather than being annihilated (Deut

10.10ff). The Gibeonites sought peace through deception and ended up in subservience, as 'hewers of wood and drawers of water' (Josh 9.23).

A very challenging use of *shalom* is found in 2 Sam 11.7, where David sends for Uriah, the husband of Bathsheba, and inquires of him about the *shalom* of Joab, the *shalom* of the people, and the *shalom* of the war (three times *shalom*!) The Revised Standard Version (RSV) reads: 'David asked how Joab was doing, and how the people fared, and how the war prospered.' But, more accurately, David inquired about the *shalom* of the war! Is this a war called peace?

As Solomon's prosperity and power increased he is said to have had *shalom* on all sides (see, e.g., 1 Kings 4.25; 5.12). But we discover the cost of this questionable 'peace' as 1 Kings 9.15–24 informs us about the forced labour for Solomon's extravagant building programme, which was certainly not *shalom*, and the taxes levelled to finance the 'force of chariots and horses' (Jerusalem Bible). This was a professional army of one thousand four hundred chariots (imported from Egypt), and twelve thousand horsemen (among whom were probably some foreign 'advisers'!), whom he lodged in 'chariot cities' (1 Kings 10.26–29).

Another striking story is found in 2 Kings 9, which relates how Jehu overthrew the house of Ahab. The prophet Elisha, the man of God, instigated the coup by having Jehu, who was called 'commander' by his companions (2 Kings 9.5), anointed as King by one of his disciples, although he had no linear claim to the throne. At first Jehu's companions were suspicious, and asked, 'Is all well (*shalom*)?' but acclaimed Jehu as their king as soon as they heard the whole story. As Jehu rushed to Jezreel, King Joram sent a messenger inquiring, 'Is it peace (*shalom*)?', to which Jehu replied, 'What have you to do with peace (*shalom*)?' (2 Kings 9.18). Then King Joram of Israel and Ahaziah of Judah set out together by chariot to meet Jehu. When they met him, Joram again said, 'Is it peace (*shalom*), Jehu?' He answered, 'What peace can there be, so long as the harlotries and the sorceries of your mother Jezebel are so many!' (2 Kings 9.22–23). Both kings were killed as they fled, and Joram's corpse was thrown into the vineyard of Naboth, which had been confiscated fraudulently by Ahab, Joram's father, upon the instigation of Jezebel (1 Kings 21). As Jehu entered Jezreel, Jezebel said, 'Is it peace (*shalom*), you Zimri, murderer of your master?' But Jehu ordered her to be thrown out of the window by her servants (2 Kings 9.31–33).

Peace is not so much the opposite of war as of injustice, as can be seen for instance in Jer 6.13–14 (= Jer 8.10–11):

> . . . from the least to the greatest of them
> every one is greedy for unjust gain;
> and from prophet to priest every one deals falsely.
> They have healed the wound of my people lightly,
> saying, 'Peace, peace,'
> when there is no peace.

These verses assail the general corruption of the people, particularly the clergy who, greedy for gain, lull the nation into a false sense of security. They go around saying, 'Peace, peace', while there is no peace, since they do not remove the root causes of injustice which make true peace impossible.

Prophetic struggle for *shalom*

During the time of the Judges God raised up liberators entrusted with regaining *shalom* which Israel time and again lost through its transgressions. For some time David (2 Sam 7.1) and Solomon (1 Chron 22.9) were thought to incorporate the same liberating ideal. But this ideal very quickly became corrupted and the kings sought to acquire peace for themselves, not as the fruit of justice but by means of political intrigues and alliances, supported in these efforts by false prophets. 'Then I said, Ah, Lord God, behold, the prophets say to them, "You shall not see the sword, nor shall you have famine, but I will give you assured peace in this place." And the Lord said to me, "The prophets are prophesying lies in my name. I did not send them . . ."' (Jer 14.13–14).

Towards 850 BC Micah entered into dispute with these false prophets about the word and the reality of peace (1 Kings 22.23–28). The struggle reached a climax during the siege of Jerusalem (see Jer 23.9–40). The gift of peace would require suppression of injustice, which caused Ezekiel to cry out: 'Enough whitewashings! The walls must fall' (Ezek 13.15f.). But later God announced to the Exiles: 'I know the plans I have for you, plans for welfare (*shalom*) and not for evil, to give you a future and a hope' (Jer 29.11). A covenant of peace would be concluded, assuring security and blessing (Ezek 34.25–3Ո); for, said God, 'I will be with them' (Ezek 37.26).

This concern with *shalom* was shared by all the prophets and eventually became an essential element in their preaching about God's plans for the future. Their threatening oracles usually ended with an announcement of abundant restoration to follow (Hos 2.20; Amos 9.13, etc.).

According to Isaiah this restoration of peace will be accomplished through the sacrifice of God's suffering Servant (Isa 53.5). But Isaiah also indicates what the price of peace will be: the Servant will lay down his life for all. Then it will be truly, 'Peace, peace, to the far and to the near . . . and I will heal them' (Isa 57.19). 'I will make your overseers peace and your taskmasters justice. Violence shall no more be heard in your land . . .' (Isa 60.17–18).[1]

The covenant of *shalom*

The root of *berith*, 'covenant', is 'to cut', referring to the solemn covenant ritual of passing between the divided parts of slaughtered animals (Gen 15.10, 18; Jer 34.18). Eating together was also basic to *berith*. A covenant could be between individuals (1 Sam 18.3; 23.18). Marriage is described as a covenant (Mal 2.14). Kings made covenants (2 Sam 8.9–10; 1 Kings 20.34), and a king could make a covenant with his people (2 Kings 11.4). Tribes and nations could also make covenants (Josh 9.6).

A covenant entailed rights and obligations, and the parties involved were not always on an equal footing. Often it involved an exchange of gifts, and accepting a gift placed a person or community under obligation.

The Bible contains many references to the covenant God made with his people and which contained promises and obligations. *Berith* and *shalom* are frequently linked so that the phrase 'covenant of *shalom*' becomes almost an official term, *shalom* conveying the character and quality of the covenant. A covenant of *shalom* should result in *shalom* in the widest and deepest sense.

Shalom and salvation

Many of the features of *shalom* discussed above are closely related to the Hebrew perception of salvation, which is God's gift and action on behalf of his people. Thus salvation was experienced first and foremost in the exodus events.

Salvation means victory in the struggles of liberation from evil individuals, groups, and nations, but also the acquisition of well-being and happiness. Salvation means victory in the courts of justice, as well as the blessings of rain and fertility. Hence, the concept of salvation and *shalom* are intertwined. People who are persecuted by their enemies (Ps 7.2; 40.14–15; 59.3), who are oppressed and plundered (Deut 28.29–31), who suffer misery and hunger (Ps 34.7), all long for salvation, a happy state in which they will be freed from all forms of evil.

So, salvation, like *shalom*, denotes wholeness and integrity. The covenant was supposed to provide all this; but time and again the people broke the covenant which resulted in the removal of *shalom* and the resurgence of disunity, distrust, alienation, poverty, the oppression of one person or group by another, or the whole people by a foreign power. Yet even in the darkest moments there remained an openness to the future, a future which would not be the result of people's schemes but a gift of God.

Shalom and sacrifice

The meaning of the phrase 'peace offering' (*zebah*

selamim), or 'sacrifice(s) of peace offering(s),' which appears in the Torah and especially in Leviticus and Numbers (about sixty times) is obscure. *Zebah* means something that is slain or slaughtered and refers, therefore, to a slain sacrificial victim. *Selamin* is derived from the root *slm*, from which is also derived *shalom*, 'peace', which means 'to be complete', 'to be whole', 'to be in harmony'. The designation 'peace offering' seems to be derived from the Septuagint (the Greek Old Testament) and falls somehow short of the original idea. One suggestion is that it means 'fulfilment offering', 'offering of completeness', or 'final offering'. Although the precise meaning of the Hebrew expression remains obscure, it certainly involves the preservation of harmonious relationships between participants in the sacrifice and Yahweh, as portrayed especially in the common meal.

Shalom as 'peace of mind'?

Gerhard von Rad maintains that there are no instances in the Old Testament where *shalom* would refer to the psychological condition of inner peace.

> When we consider the rich possibilities of *shalom* in the Old Testament we are struck by the negative fact that there is no specific text in which it denotes the specifically spiritual attitude of inward peace. There are, indeed, more passages in which it is used of groups rather than individuals . . . it manifests itself in the form of external well-being. In the majority of examples, in which the reference is to a group, the term *shalom* clearly denotes something which may be seen . . . we are forced to say that in its most common use *shalom* is an emphatically social concept.[2]

Conclusion

According to von Rad,

> We constrict the term *shalom* if we equate it with
> 'peace'. At root it means 'well-being', with a strong
> emphasis on the material side. In meetings or letters
> well-being is wished to others, and in conversations
> one asks about their well-being . . . In many . . .
> instances *shalom* really signifies bodily health or well-
> being and the related satisfaction. More commonly
> *shalom* is referred to a group, eg, a nation enjoying
> prosperity. This brings us closer to the thought of
> peace . . . Yet, here too, there are many cases where
> *shalom* means something more fundamental than our
> 'peace', . . . ie, to be concerned for the *shalom*, the
> well-being of the people. This brings us to the great
> number of passages in which *shalom* denotes a rela-
> tionship rather than a state . . . The relationship may
> be that of a people . . . It may naturally exist between
> individuals too . . . Since the Hebrews sometimes use
> *berith* for this kind of alliance, it is not surprising that
> *shalom* occurs when there is reference to a covenant.
> Indeed, the connection between the two words is so
> strong that in this context *shalom* seems to have
> become a kind of official term. The thought may be
> that the relationship of *shalom* is sealed by both
> parties in a covenant. Conversely, it may be that the
> covenant inaugurates a relationship of *shalom*.[3]

B. Peace in the Greek Bible (eirene)

The Graeco-Roman World

The basic feature of the Greek concept of *eirene* is that,

unlike in Hebrew, the word does not primarily denote a relationship between several persons (and between those persons and God). Rather, it denotes a state, a condition, ie a 'time of peace' or a 'state of peace', originally thought of primarily as an interval in a continuous state of war. In Greek thought, therefore, again unlike in Hebrew thought, peace is the opposite of war. *Eirene* is the state of peace from which flow all blessings for both land and people, and which is considered the supreme good.

Eirene also refers especially to the prevailing condition in the Graeco-Roman world during the reign of Emperor Augustus (27 BC–AD 14), during which Jesus was born. There was a very strong longing for *redemption*, and pacification was achieved by the strong hand of the Emperor, with the result that in everyday reality *eirene* implied the legal *security* of the pax Romana.[4]

The Septuagint

The Hebrew word *shalom* is mostly translated by *eirene* in the Septuagint. (This refers to the Greek version of the Old Testament, translated for the Library of Alexandria in Egypt just before 200 BC, on which seventy scholars (Greek *septuaginta*, 'seventy') are said to have worked.) To be exact, seven Hebrew words are translated in the Septuagint by *eirene*, but five of them only once each. The sixth word, *batah*, which means 'trust', 'confidence', 'security', is tendered by *eirene* nine times. In all other instances *eirene* corresponds to *shalom* and its cognate forms in the Hebrew Bible.

The use of *eirene* as the Greek equivalent of *shalom* caused some change in the concept of peace, as *eirene* carried the ideas associated with it in the Graeco-Roman world. But although most of the early Christians would have used the Septuagint rather than the Hebrew Bible, for them the word *eirene* would also have carried the ideas associated with *shalom*.

Hence in many passages in the Greek Bible *eirene* means the prosperity or salvation of people. This may be expressed in the form of an introductory greeting, 'Peace be to you' (Judg 6.23), or in the form of a farewell, 'Go in peace. The journey on which you go is under the eye of the Lord' (Judg 18.6). It may be an inquiry as to someone's welfare, 'Is it well (*eirene*) with the young Absolom?' (2 Sam 18.29), or a matter of going or returning 'in peace' (Gen 26.29).

Eirene can refer to the total well-being of people: 'Great is the Lord who delights in the welfare (*eirene*) of his servant' (Ps 35.27). The term easily moves from the meaning of concrete prosperity to the more general-meaning of good: 'Her (Wisdom's) ways are ways of pleasantness, and all her paths are peace' (Prov 3.17). Hence *eirene* can be used to indicate the good which comes from God, both in the present age and in the age of salvation. In fact, *eirene* can signify this divinely given good in any sphere of life: 'I am the Lord . . . I make weal (*eirene*, well-being) and create woe . . .' (Isa 45.7).

C. Conclusion

We conclude this chapter on *shalom/eirene* in the Old Testament by quoting a moving description of peace found in Micah 4.3–4:

. . . and they shall beat their swords into ploughshares, and their spears into pruning hooks;

nation shall not lift up sword against nation,
neither shall they learn war anymore;
but they shall sit every man under his vine
and under his fig tree,
and none shall make them afraid;
for the mouth of the Lord of hosts has spoken.

Note on Rabbinic Literature

Shalom is used extensively in Rabbinic literature. It is used as a greeting and as part of a farewell, and it is used in the sense of well-being. Like the Old Testament the Rabbis also used *shalom* for the gift of God to his people. It also refers to peace as opposed to strife between individuals or nations. Consequently, there are frequent references to the making of peace between people.

Discussion Questions

1. Discuss the Old Testament concept of peace (*shalom*). In what respects does it differ from our present-day concept? In what respects is it similar?

2. Is *shalom* the opposite of war? Why?/Why not?

3. How do you evaluate the prophetic struggle for peace?

4. How is *shalom* related to the Covenant?/to Salvation?

5. Does *shalom* have the same meaning as the word 'peace' in the expression 'peace and order'?

6. In what respects did the Greek concept of peace differ from *shalom* in the Hebrew Bible?

7. How have the Hebrew and Greek concepts of peace
   influenced the early Christians' concept of peace?
   our present-day concept?

2. Peace in the Gospels and Acts

The word *eirene* is found once in Mark (Mk 5.34), four times in Matthew (Mt 10.13, 34 twice each), twelve or thirteen times in Luke (Lk 24.36 is doubtful), six times in John, and seven times in the Acts of the Apostles. As for the whole of the New Testament, the meaning of *eirene* in the Gospels and Acts is much the same as that of the Rabbinic *shalom*, as can be seen first of all in its use in greetings and similar expressions where it means well-being and salvation; e.g., 'go in peace' (Mk 5.34 par. Lk 8.48; Lk 7.50), and greetings on arrival, such as 'peace be to –' (Lk 10.5; Jn 20.19, 21, 26). 'Lord, now let your servant depart in peace' (Lk 2.29) has basically the same meaning. *Eirene* in the sense of security may be found in Lk 11.21: 'When a strong man, fully armed, guards his own palace, his goods are in peace.' Generally speaking, it is not the Greek meaning of the word which predominates in the New Testament, but the Old Testament and Rabbinic meaning of salvation in the deeper sense – the salvation promised by God (Lk 1.79; 2.14; 19.42).

'On earth peace among men' (Lk 2.14)

This verse in Luke's infancy narrative (Lk 1.5—2.52) was and still is often understood in terms of God promising peace to people who give signs of good will; hence a lot of cheap talk about 'men of good will', especially at

Christmas. Scholars now agree that 'good will' or 'good pleasure' in this verse is a quality attributed to God rather than to 'men'. Peace is promised to people with whom God is well pleased – peace in the biblical sense, that is, not superficial harmony concealing a lot of injustice and inequality.

The Emperor Augustus appropriated the title Saviour, which the Bible attributes to God only, and claimed to have established the *pax Romana* throughout the empire. The birth of a son to an emperor was 'good news of joy' fulfilling ancient hopes. Over and against these claims Luke announced the birth of Jesus as 'good news of joy'. Jesus, then, is the real Saviour, born in the insignificant town of Bethlehem instead of in Rome (Lk 2.11); and his birth is the dawning of real peace – i.e., wholeness in relation with God, people, the physical world, and oneself.

Luke-Acts, with one exception, reflects this context. The messianic salvation is described as the way of peace (1.79). Jesus Christ is said to have preached the good news of peace (Acts 10.36). This peace associated with God's acts in Jesus involves recovered wholeness in the relation of a person with God (e.g. Lk 7.50), wholeness in the relation with the physical world (8.48), and wholeness in the relations among persons (e.g., Acts 9.31). The absence of any reference to peace with oneself is not surprising in Luke-Acts both because of the evangelist's focus on the visible and external realities of life, and because the Scriptures on which Luke is so dependent have little concern with peace as an inward feeling. For Jesus' birth to be connected with the recovery of peace, therefore, was a matter of great joy, meaning the restoration of wholeness to life in every area: with God, with others, with the physical world. It is this peace about which the heavenly choir sings at 2.14.[5]

One may say that with the mention of good news, Saviour, and peace, Luke presents here a kind of 'anti-emperor ideology', whereby he denies the emperor's claims and substitutes God's and Jesus' claims for them. No emperor, no king, no president, no chairman will bring about 'peace', but only God in and through Jesus.

'I have not come to bring peace' (Mt 10.34; Lk 12.51)

Since this saying appears in a somewhat different form in Matthew and Luke we first present the texts in parallel:

Matthew 10.34	Luke 12.51
Do not think that I have come to bring peace on earth; I have not come to bring peace, but a sword.	Do you think that I have come to give peace on earth? No, I tell you, but rather division.

As one commentator has pointed out,

> Quoted out of context – as they often are – these verses seem more appropriate to the Qu'ran than to the Gospels; they sound like a cry of Muhammad proclaiming a Jihad or holy war, rather than a genuine utterance of the Prince of Peace.[6]

The peace which in this verse Jesus is said not to bring on earth is neither peace in Israel, nor between nations, nor between God and man. Both Jesus himself and the apostolic proclamation concerning him divide society into two camps. Luke's version has 'division' instead of 'sword', and this correctly expresses the thought. This indicates that the 'sword' is to be interpreted in this context in a figurative rather than a literal sense. It is quite often thought to refer to persecution 'on account of the gospel', but more probably it refers to division. The mission and message of Jesus produce division: people are divided by reason of their response to him. The sword is therefore metaphorical: it is the instrument that divides families. The *effects* produced by Jesus' preaching are presented as the *purpose* for which Jesus came. This is a typically Hebrew way of presenting things. (Compare Mk 4.11–12 where it is said that Jesus spoke in parables 'so that they may indeed see and not perceive', although Mark is speaking of the effects or the result of Jesus' preaching.)

The *ultimate* effect of Jesus' coming on earth may be reconciliation to God and enduring peace; but the *immediate* effect of his proclamation is often division and conflict.

In the following verses (Mt 10.35–36/Lk 12.52–53) these divisive effects are expressed by means of an adaptation of an oracle found in Micah 7.1–7. This oracle originally dealt with the total breakdown of moral life in Israel, in domestic as well as public relations, but is here used to say that Jesus' proclamation can cause hostility and division within one and the same family, between those who accept and those who reject his message. The text speaks of a division of loyalties within the family.

This theme was anticipated in Luke's infancy narrative: 'Behold, this child is set for the fall and rising of many in Israel, and for a sign that is spoken against (and a sword will pierce through your own soul also), that thoughts out of many hearts may be revealed' (Lk 2.34–35). The call for decision is a call for 'division'!

Though peace is an important effect of the Christ-event in the Lucan view, the evangelist has here retained . . . an interpretation of Jesus' ministry in terms of its opposite. Yet even that effect of his ministry has been foreshadowed in the infancy narrative: Jesus was a child set 'for the fall and rise of many in Israel' (2.34). He now spells out a mode which that discord may take: division within families . . . The Lucan Jesus has come during the era of Augustan peace, as a sign of peace among human beings; he has not come as the fiery reformer that John once expected . . . Yet his ministry is now described by him as a source of discord among the very people he came to serve and save.[7]

One does not get rid of the difficulty of Matthew's harsh term 'sword' by describing it as purely figurative for while 'division' may imply 'conflict' but not necessarily 'violence', the 'sword' has all its associations with violent conflict and with the use of the armed hand . . . If we can take Mt 26.52–53 as authentic dominical utterances, then they do not only make it abundantly clear that Jesus dissociated himself absolutely from political zealotry, but at the same time (verse 53) would seem to imply belief in the possibility of the intervention in the destiny of the world of 'legions of angels', a heavenly warrior host, exactly as in the apocalyptic war of the Sons of Light with the Sons of Darkness . . . While not a political Zealot, Jesus could perhaps be claimed as an apocalyptic Zealot, proclaiming a final impending war against Belial and all his followers in heaven and on earth, even in the same family. The sword would then be an image of this terrible prelude to the last judgment, the manifestation of the wrath of God by the armies of heaven.[8]

'Blessed are the peacemakers' (Mt 5.9)

The seventh beatitude is addressed to the peace*makers*, not peace*keepers*. The Greek word *eirenopoios*, 'he who makes peace', is found only here in the whole of the Greek Bible. The verb *eirenopoiein*, 'to make peace', also appears only once in the New Testament (Col 1.20). But we find it also in the Old Testament, more particularly in Proverbs 10.10, which in the Greek Bible differs from the Hebrew and says: 'he who boldly reproves makes peace.' This text proves very important in determining the true meaning of 'peacemakers'. It shows indeed that 'peacemakers' does not mean 'those who keep their peace', or those who keep quiet. No, peacemakers are people who commit themselves actively to bring about peace. Many a peace*keeper* ultimately succeeds only in causing more trouble and not peace, allowing a threatening and dangerous situation to drag on, and defending himself by saying that for sake of peace he does not want to take action. In contrast, the peace of which the Bible speaks is not achieved by evading issues, but by facing them and effectively dealing with them, even if this involves a certain amount of confrontation and struggle.

The beatitude is addressed to those who commit themselves actively to bring about peace in the biblical sense of the general well-being of the community in which all equally benefit. This condition is impossible without a solid substratum of *justice*. So, the struggle for justice, provided it is really a struggle for justice for all, and not just for one sector in society – not an inversion of the pyramid, so that the oppressed become oppressors and the oppressors oppressed – is truly peacemaking.

The peacemakers 'shall be called sons of God'. In a biblical-semitic way of speaking, 'to be called' means 'to be'. The passive refers to God's action and should be understood to mean that God will call them. When God calls somebody something, he makes that person what he calls him. Compare 1 Jn 3.1: 'See what love the Father has given us, that we should *be called* children of God; and so we *are*.' To be a 'son of God' means to be accepted in the peace and friendship of God, to be close to God.

It should now be clear that the peace in *peace*makers, as elsewhere in the Bible, is very different from the peace mentioned in the expression 'peace and order'. If you want to see the ideal of what people who speak of 'peace and order' have in mind, visit a cemetery! There everything is quiet, nobody protests! This is not biblical peace.

Discussion Questions

1. What is the meaning of 'on earth peace among men' (Lk 2.14)?

2. What does 'I have not come to bring peace but a sword' (Mt 10.34) mean?

3. Discuss the beatitude of the peacemakers (Mt 5.9).

4. What is the difference between peace*makers* and peace*keepers*?

3. Peace in Pauline Literature

Out of ninety-one occurrences in the New Testament the word *eirene* is found forty-three times in Pauline literature, especially Romans (ten times) and Ephesians (eight times), and in the other letters between one and three times each.

'Grace to you and peace . . .'

All Pauline letters begin with the greeting 'Grace to you and peace from God our Father and the Lord Jesus Christ' (except 1 Thess: 'Grace to you and peace', and 1 and 2 Tim: 'Grace, mercy and peace from God the Father and Christ Jesus our Lord'). This greeting formula is unknown prior to the New Testament, and seems to have been created by the early Church, perhaps even by Paul himself.

The customary Greek form of address in a letter occurs in Acts 23.26: 'Claudius Lysias to his Excellency the governor Felix, greeting.' The Greek word for 'greeting(s)' is *chairein*, literally 'rejoice'. Paul exchanged the word *charis*, 'grace', for *chairein*. Both words have a similar sound and are derived from the same root. But *charis* is not just a standard greeting term. It is equivalent to the frequently used Hebrew term *hen*, which means 'favour'. With its connotation of God's favour to Israel, this word comes to mean, in the New Testament, God's free love for us as manifested in

Jesus. This is Paul's wish for those he addresses.

To this Paul added 'peace', equivalent to the Hebrew greeting *shalom*, which stands for wholeness, health, harmony, and prosperity. It is a gift of God made available through the saving ministry of his Son. The 'peace' thus realized is the final and decisive salvation of the whole person and the whole community.

'Peace' is the result of 'grace', God's loving and gratuitous initiative. He is the 'God of peace' (Rom 15.33; 2 Cor 13.11; Phil 4.9; 1 Thess 5.23), and the gospel preaching is the 'gospel of peace' (Eph 6.15)

Today the word 'peace' is used primarily in two senses. First, it can mean the absence of war or strife among nations, groups, or individuals. Second, it can mean an interior tranquillity marked by freedom from anxiety – peace of mind. These meanings are not entirely absent from Pauline literature, but they are rare. Predominant in the Pauline conception of peace is neither external harmony nor inner serenity, but rather the idea of messianic salvation. This is rooted in the Old Testament, but enriched by the overpowering reality of Christ's saving death and resurrection. For Paul 'peace' is seen in relationship to God, as especially developed in Romans, and in relationship to our fellow human beings, as developed in Ephesians.

Romans: Reconciliation with God

All human beings are sinners who 'fall short of the glory of God' (Rom 3.23) and are unable to become 'righteous' by their own efforts: 'But now the righteousness of God has been manifested apart from law, although the law and the prophets bear witness to it, the righteousness of God through faith in Jesus Christ for all who believe' (Rom 3.21–22). So, God has taken the initiative. In Rom 5 Paul begins to develop the effects of this righteousness, which is God's free gift: 'Therefore, since we are justified by faith, we have *peace* with God through our Lord Jesus Christ. Through him we have obtained access to this grace in which we stand, and we rejoice in our hope of sharing in the glory of God' (Rom 5.1–2).

The 'peace' which we enjoy as a result of justification is much more than freedom from fear, or inner 'peace of mind'. The change we have experienced is not just a change in how we *feel*; it is a change in the *reality* of our relationship to God. Christ is the channel through whom we have both 'peace' and 'access to this grace in which we stand'. Here, as in Paul's greeting formula, grace and peace are once more connected.

Paul refers to this experience also as reconciliation: 'For if while we were enemies we were reconciled to God by the death of his Son, much more, now that we are reconciled, shall we be saved by his life' (Rom 5.10). Thus God alone is the author of peace, which consists in a restoration of humanity's right relation to God.

Ephesians: Reconciliation with others

The author of Ephesians, most probably a disciple of Paul, also writes about the removal of hostility as reconciliation and making peace. But he carries the reflection a step further: there was not only hostility between God and humankind, but also between Jew and Gentile. Therefore, he takes up the question of establishing peace within humankind, and states that this reconciliation too derives from the saving ministry of Christ.

Addressing Christians of Gentile origin, Eph 2.14–18

says that they are no longer 'strangers', but have received equal standing with the chosen people. This idea is based on Isa 57.19: 'Peace, peace, to the far and to the near, says the Lord.' The 'far' are taken to be the Gentiles, the 'near' the Jews. The promise of 'peace' to both has been fulfilled in Christ's redeeming work,

> that he might create in himself one new man in place of the two, so *making peace*, and might reconcile us both to God in one body through the cross, thereby bringing the hostility to an end. And he came and preached *peace* to you who were far off and *peace* to those who were near; for through him we both have access in one Spirit to the Father (Eph 2.15–18).

We cannot be reconciled with God without at the same time being reconciled with each other. This is also realized by Christ who 'is our *peace*, who has made us both one, and has broken down the dividing wall of hostility . . . so making *peace*' (Eph 2.14–15). This restoration of relationships within humankind is a gift. It is not something we achieve, but something that has basically already been achieved for us by the Father through Christ in the Spirit.

As any other time in history, our time is very much in need of the breaking down of barriers, which is the great creator of prejudice, of which no country or race or culture is free.

> It is a vicious kind of mental slant pushed up out of your culture that makes up your mind for you before you think. It is an evil kind of mental blind spot that shuts from your view the facts of a given situation. It is a tyrannous mental fence that holds you from friendships you need and confines you to your own backyard. It may be racial, religious, sectional, econo-

mic, or social. It is always personal, and in some sense it is always cultural. It is a symptom of pride, ignorance, and ego anywhere it happens to you, and it cuts across justice, perverts the truth, subsists on lies, and worse; it twists and wastes personality, for whose sake culture exists to begin with.[9]

Peace as a responsibility

For all his insistence on 'peace', Paul also warns his readers about a false and deceptive understanding of this reality: 'When people say, "There is peace and security," then sudden destruction will come upon them as travail comes upon a woman with child, and there will be no escape' (1 Thess 5.3). This statement cannot be a direct reference to the parousia – i.e. the (second) coming of Christ – since Paul 'introduces the statement with a word (*otan*) which indicates iteration and conditionality and puts *say* in the present tense, "as often as men say" .'[10] Paul's statement is most probably influenced by Jer 6.14 (see Chapter 1). The theme of sudden destruction in the midst of supposed security is also found in Lk 17.26/Mt 24.37–39 which refer to the disasters that struck humankind in the time of Noah and Lot. Paul, then, is speaking of disaster striking people who live with a false sense of peace and security here and now.

[The] perspective, that peace with God and among ourselves is a *given*, so dominates Pauline thought that little is said explicitly about peace as something yet to be done, as a task for us to accomplish. The victory is won; what remains is simply the mopping-up operations. Yet there are two lines of thought in Paul that may be extended to show that the task of making peace is implicit in his teaching.[11]

Firstly, there is the tension between the 'already' and the 'not yet'. Our peace with God and with one another has already been basically established, but it has not been completely developed. It is not yet a full reality either in our personal life or in the society around us. Hence the urgent task of peace-making.

Secondly, there is Paul's treatment of the 'ministry of reconciliation': 'All this is from God who through Christ reconciled us to himself *and gave us the ministry of reconciliation*; that is, God was in Christ reconciling the world to himself . . . and *entrusting to us the message of reconciliation*' (2 Cor 5.18–19).

> Peace, like other aspects of the kingdom of God, shares fully in the tension between the 'already' and the 'not yet', the Christian paradox. The task of the peacemaker is that of trying to reduce the gap between the 'not yet' and the 'already'.[12]

Peace-making does not consist in giving people false hopes or a deceiving sense of peace and security, be it on political, economic, or pseudo-religious grounds. This would indeed be opium of the people! No, peace-making consists in facing and tackling the obstacles of injustice and sin in general, which make peace in the real biblical sense impossible, and challenging others to become committed to the same task: the task of working towards a situation of total well-being in the community in which *all* – not a 'class', no matter what the name of that class may be – equally benefit.

Discussion Questions

1. Discuss the biblical concept of reconciliation. Does it have the same meaning as it has in appeals of oppressed persons or groups for reconciliation?

2. What do you understand by 'ministry of reconciliation'?

4. Peace in the General Epistles and Revelation

Eirene, 'peace', occurs eleven times in the General Epistles (i.e. the seven New Testament letters which are not Pauline, and which were given the title 'general' or 'catholic', presumably because they were addressed to the whole Christian Church and not to particular communities or individuals). The word is found twice in the Book of Revelation or the Apocalypse.

James: Peace and justice

In the first part of his second chapter (Jas 2.1–13),

> James, like Jesus, now blows the whistle on name-dropping, now-it's-their-turn syndromes, snobbery, catering to society's exploitative structures, and indulgence of accepted neighborhood standards of oppression. To judge from his choice of diction here and elsewhere in his essay, it appears that James aims to reach a cross-section of Christendom – city and country dwellers, farmers and tradespeople, with an admixture of slaves. Oppressed and exploited people easily fall into the trap of patronizing and encouraging the very institutions they abhor. One of the religious anomalies of history is the patent classification of congregations, and in some instances entire Church bodies, along class lines . . . Much of the world's injustice is in fact traceable to the sin of partiality

depicted in 2.1–4; for the definition of 'neighbour' is left to arbitrary choice, and justice succumbs to private preference. Partiality or respect of persons prompts citizens to close their eyes to illegal actions that impose continuing hardship on the poor and the powerless, who lack the clout of expensive judicial process or well-financed lobbies . . . *Integrity of the believer's profession of faith* has been our author's theme thus far. Self-advertised religious claim is to be accompanied by quality performance levels. Now in 2.14–23 James makes his point as clear as the water of Siberian Lake Baikal. But a word of caution. One will miss his meaning and lapse into trivial moralizing if James' scenario is taken as a vignette out of actual congregational life. Exaggerated illustration and rapierlike dialogue were typical features of the ancient philosophical-homiletical argumentative form known as *diatribe* . . . The impact of our essayist's illustrations begins to be felt when one realizes that only a sadistic idiot would in real life perpetrate the kind of dialogue presented in 2.16.[13]

James 2.16–17 reads: 'If a brother or sister is ill-clad and in lack of daily food, and one of you says to them, "Go in peace, be warmed and filled," without giving them the things needed for the body, what does it profit?' Just as well-wishing without any effective assistance is worthless, so faith without praxis is worthless. If a brother or sister has nothing to wear and nothing to eat, he or she is afflicted by the two great concerns of life (see Mt 6.25–34/Lk 12.22–31). Instead of caring for them, the character of this little 'parable' gets rid of them with a formalistic, 'go in peace', or 'good luck to you'. It signals the end of the encounter. The formulation of the Greek text suggests that this lack of solidarity was not accidental, but protracted and deliberate.

'And the harvest of righteousness [justice] is sown in *peace* by those who make *peace*' (Jas 3.18). This verse, which may well have been a proverbial saying, concludes chapter three, the first part of which, Jas 3.1–12, deals with the use of the tongue, and the second, Jas 3.13–18, with the idea that instead of rushing to the teacher's chair, Christians should teach by their praxis, by the example of their actions. Though the general meaning of Jas 3.18 and its connection with the preceding is clear, its exact meaning is a little obscure. The 'harvest of righteousness' can mean either the 'fruit that righteousness produces' or the 'fruit that is righteousness'. The second meaning is to be preferred. 'The fruit of righteousness/justice' is an expression often found in the Bible. For example, Isaiah declares that '*justice* will dwell in the wilderness, and *righteousness* abide in the fruitful field. And the effect of *righteousness* will be *peace* . . .' (Isa 32.16–18); and Amos chides the 'great house' of the king and his cronies, who have 'turned *justice* into poison and the fruit of righteousness into wormwood [a bitter fruit]' (Amos 6.12). 'Sown in peace by those who make peace' reminds us of Mt 5.9: 'Blessed are the peacemakers . . .' (see Chapter 2). And so we may conclude that, for James, 'Peace in the community . . . is the sum of the matter of doing justice.'[14]

Peter: The search for peace

The initial greeting of both letters expresses the wish that 'grace and peace may be multiplied to you' (1 Pet 1.2; 2 Pet 1.2). 'Grace and peace' is found in all Pauline letters, but this writer adds the characteristically Jewish prayer that grace and peace 'may . . . be multiplied', which is also found in Daniel 4.1: 'Peace be multiplied to you!' The idea of abounding peace occurs in Ps 37.11. It also occurs in Ps 72.7: 'In his days may righteousness [justice] flourish, and peace abound . . .' Here again justice and peace are placed together in the same context.

In the letters of Peter, the next occurrence of *peace* is in the context of practical advice concerning the community (1 Pet 3.8–12): 'let him turn away from evil and do right, let him *seek peace and pursue it*' (1 Pet 3.11). This is part of a free quotation from Ps 34.12–16, found in 1 Pet 3.10–12. To do justice is to seek peace and pursue it. We are reminded again of Mt 5.9: 'Blessed are the peacemakers . . .' The rabbis interpreted Ps 34.14, 'seek peace and pursue it' to mean that the quest for peace was so urgent that all were to pursue it, no matter what this search would demand from them.

1 Peter ends with the blessing, 'Peace to all of you that are in Christ' (1 Pet 5.14). The members of the community are described as being 'in Christ', suggesting that the 'peace' which the author prays may be theirs is grounded in their relationship with Christ. It has been suggested that the words used here may reflect a form of blessing given at the close of sermons.

In the concluding section of 2 Peter (3.14–18), the author exhorts his readers: 'Therefore, beloved, since you wait for these [new heavens and a new earth], be zealous to be found by him without a spot or blemish, and at peace' (1 Pet 3.14). To be 'at peace' here does not denote so much the untroubled conscience (peace of mind) of the good Christians, but rather the state of reconciliation with God reflected in the restoration of harmony among all in the community. They should 'be zealous'; i.e., they should make efforts to be thus found by the Lord at his coming. So, 'waiting' here is not like waiting for your turn in a dentist's waiting room, but active involvement in the search for peace.

John: The gift of peace

We propose to deal here with the five Johannine writings: the fourth Gospel, the three letters of John, and the book of Revelation. In Jn 20.19, 21, 26 the risen Christ greets his disciples with the assurance, 'Peace be with you.' By his death and resurrection Jesus has achieved the restoration and wholeness contained in the Hebrew word *shalom*. 'Grace [mercy] and peace' is the greeting found at the beginning of the second and third letters of John and the book of Revelation.

The most important statements on peace are found in the so-called Farewell Discourse (Jn 14—17). The first and most important of all is found in Jn 14.1–31 in which Jesus answers Peter's question, 'Where are you going?' (Jn 13.36). Jesus goes to the Father (Jn 14.1–11); his earthly mission will be accomplished through his disciples (Jn 14.12–14), with the help of 'another Counsellor' (Jn 14.15–17); they will not be separated from him, but will share in his own relationship with the Father (Jn 14.18–24); and all this is made known to the disciples to sustain them at the time of Jesus' death (Jn 14.25–31). In this last paragraph we read: 'Peace I leave with you; my peace I give to you; not as the world gives do I give to you. Let not your hearts be troubled, neither let them be afraid.'

The peace of which Jesus speaks has nothing to do with the absence of war . . . nor with an end to psychological tension, nor with a sentimental feeling of well-being . . . In Johannine language 'peace', 'truth', 'light', 'life', and 'joy' are figurative terms reflecting different facets of the great gift that Jesus brought from the Father to men. 'Peace is my gift to you' is another way of saying 'I give them eternal life' (10.28). The 'my peace' of which Jesus speaks here is the same as 'my joy' of 15.11; 17.13. The use of the term 'peace' here is particularly appropriate since a farewell is involved . . . The theme of peace also belongs to the covenant mentality we have seen exhibited at the Last Supper. In Ezek 37.26, Yahweh says to Ezekiel, 'I will make a covenant of peace with them.'[15]

As a valediction it is a bestowal of blessing, and so conveys a certain power which can remain with the disciples . . . So *leave* virtually means bequeath . . . In the light of the foregoing discourse, Jesus' blessing carries with it the whole positive content of the abiding effects of the Resurrection which he has described. Hence it is *not as the world gives*, a perfunctory farewell devoid of real power. Therefore Jesus can repeat the reassurance of verse 1, but even more emphatically.[16]

When the world uses 'Peace' in a greeting it expresses a hope. It can do no more. And even that it usually does in no more than a conventional sense . . . But Christ effectually gives men peace. Moreover, the peace of which He speaks is not dependent on any outward circumstances, as any peace the world can give must necessarily be. Because He gives men such a peace Jesus can enjoin them not to be troubled in heart nor cowardly.[17]

The other mention of *peace* is found in the final verse of Chapter 16: 'I have said this to you, that in me you may have peace. In the world you have tribulation; but be of good cheer, I have overcome the world' (Jn 16.33). The theme of peace which occurred in Jn 14.27 appears here too. Once again it should be stressed that peace is a *salvific gift*. The fact that it exists alongside suffering shows that it is not peace in the ordinary sense of the word. In Jn 14.29 Jesus said, 'I have told you this . . . so that . . . you may believe.' Here he says, 'I have said this to you so that in me you may find peace.' Peace flows from belief in Jesus and consists of union with him. Peace is not acquired effortlessly, for it comes only from victory over the world. 'If Jesus conquers the world, the individual Christian must also conquer the world (Rev 3.21); and this is done through faith (1 John 5.4–5).'[18]

Discussion Questions

1. Discuss the relationship of peace and justice in the Old Testament in the letter of James.

2. What do we mean by saying that peace is a 'gift'? Does that mean we cannot do anything about it?

Part Two

Violence

5. Violence in the Old Testament

An attentive reading of the Old Testament reveals that in this collection of books no other activity or condition occurs more often than violence. More than six hundred passages deal explicitly with peoples, kings or other individuals attacking and killing others; about one thousand texts speak of God's wrath which often punishes people with death and annihilation; and there are over a hundred instances in which God is said to order the killing of people.[19] Quite a number of root words in Hebrew imply violence, but the word *hamas*, currently translated as 'violence', is the most important. In addition to physical violence, this word can refer to robbery, commerical exploitation, false witness, and other forms of oppression, *but always committed by the stronger against the weaker*. The efforts of the weaker to throw off the yoke of the stronger are never called violence. In the following pages we will study the different aspects of *hamas*, 'violence'.

A. Violence (*hamas*): A Word-Study

As said above, *hamas* is the best known among the terms which in the Bible speak of oppression. Leaving aside its many other meanings we concentrate here on its reference to social injustice and oppression, convinced by a reading of the Psalms and the Prophets that this is its point of emphasis.

The root *hms*

The root *hms* is found sixty-eight times in the Old Testament, eight times in its verbal form and sixty times in its substantive form *hamas*. It is found thirty-one times in the Prophets, seventeen times in the Psalms and related literature, twelve times in Wisdom literature, six times in narrative texts, and twice in legal texts.

The victims of *hamas*

As victims of violence the Bible mentions: Israel (nine times); people suffering the violence of the kings and the ruling class (twice); an unidentified group undergoing the violence of others (nine times); the poor (seven times); the just and innocent (eight times); the stranger, the widow and the orphan (once); particular persons (twice: Job and Sarah); various other persons or things; the spouse, the trees of Lebanon, etc. (eighteen times); non-specified (twelve times). We may note that the number of texts in which specified social groups, like the poor, are mentioned is rather low. The prophets in particular rarely mentioned the victims of oppression, because they felt violence was everywhere. There can be little doubt that during the time of Amos, for example, the victims of violence and oppression were small farmers; but he and other prophets wanted it to be known that violence is a widespread social reality which increases more and more. We give here some samples:

Israel: 'The *violence* done to me and to my kinsmen be upon Babylon, let the inhabitant of Zion say' (Jer 51.35).

People: 'Thus says the Lord God: Enough, O princes of Israel! Put away *violence* and

oppression, and execute justice and righteousness; cease your evictions of people,
says the Lord God' (Ez 45.9).

Poor: 'For he delivers the needy when he calls,
the poor and him who has no helper . . .
From *oppression* and *violence* he redeems
their life' (Ps 72.12–14).

The agents of *hamas*

As perpetrators of violence the Bible mentions: the nations (fourteen times); the king and officials (three
times); groups which are not further defined (ten times);
the evil ones, like persecutors, false witnesses (seventeen times); the rich, the priests, the judges (five times);
various people, such as Abimelech (nine times); not
specified (eight times). In all these instances violence is
committed by a person or persons in a position of power.
The word 'violence' is never used for the action of a
person or persons who try or manage to overthrow an
oppressor; e.g., the overthrow and killing of King Joram
by Jehu, who was encouraged by the prophet Elisha (2
Kings 5, discussed in Chapter 1). This should be taken
into account by people who cite biblical passages in
dealing with today's questions concerning violence.
Here are some samples:

Nations: 'The *violence* done to Lebanon will
overwhelm you; the *destruction* of the
beasts will terrify you, for the blood of
men and *violence* to the earth, to cities
and all who dwell therein' (Hab 2.17).

Kings: 'Thus says the Lord: Do justice and
righteousness, and deliver from the

hand of the *oppressor* him who has been robbed. And do no wrong or *violence* to the alien, the fatherless, and the widow [the defenseless!], nor shed innocent blood in this place' (Jer 22.3).

Persecutors: 'Consider my affliction and my trouble, and forgive all my sins. Consider how many are my foes, and with what *violent hatred* they hate me' (Ps 25.18–19).

Forms of violence

Three basic forms of *hamas* can be identified: physical violence, exploitation, and abuse of the word.

Physical violence

This form of *hamas* has a variety of expressions, including military violence (war), violence against nature (questions of ecology), sexual violence, and social violence.

Jer 22.3 quoted above belongs to a section dealing with the kings (Jer 21.11—23.8) which is a summary of what is expected from the king and his aides. The king is considered morally responsible for the decisions taken by royal functionaries who administer justice as described, for instance, in Jer 26.10ff. The trilogy of the 'alien, the widow and the fatherless' is taken from Deut 24.19 and Ex 22.20–21. In this context Jeremiah introduces *hamas*, which Exodus and Deuteronomy had used in a completely different context, namely, false witness. In Jer 22.3, *hamas* is found on the road which leads from exploitation to physical bloodshed: 'to shed innocent

blood', is something Jeremiah associates with the affliction of the poor (Jer 2.34; 22.17), the widow and the
orphan (Jer 7.6; 22.3), and the prophet himself (Jer
26.15). Jeremiah witnessed an increase of 'violence',
and the king himself is warned not to commit it. Habba-
kuk (1.1–3) and Ezekiel (7.23; 8.17, going as far as
murder) concur with Jeremiah's diagnosis, and use
hamas more and more in order to refer to the *violence
used by the leaders of the people*, although it is also used
to describe all forms of oppression and injustice. The
situation can be summed up by the statement: 'The
country is full of violence' (Gen 6.11).

As far as *war* is specifically concerned, we may say the
following. When Habakkuk wants to describe the
Babylonian invasion, he uses *hamas*, 'violence' (Hab
1.9): it is the first shock of oppression by the enemy, the
violence of a brutal state. Already before Habakkuk, in
one of the oldest texts of the Old Testament, *hamas*
designates the cursed act of Simeon and Levi (Gen
49.5). Gen 49, a colourful presentation of the twelve
tribes, does not lack allusions to the use of force (Gen
49.9, 19, 24, 27), but these actions which we would
qualify as 'violent' are not presented as worthy of blame.
It is the anger, the frenzy, the brutality (Gen 49.7)
leading to wanton killing and mutilation (Gen 49.6),
which makes the actions of Simeon and Levi into an
example of *hamas*. The excesses of the two tribes
threaten the balance which allows all to survive and live
together. Their action incurs the only malediction
uttered by Jacob. Their violence turns against them.

Later, in the time of the Judges, it is not anger and
frenzy, but the cold political calculation which leads
Abimelech to kill his seventy brothers, which is qualified
as *hamas* (Judg 9.24). It is treason: he murders his

brothers (Judg 9.5, 24, 56) employing the tactics of surprise and deceit.

Hamas is not a neutral act: it destroys the right order of things, and disrupts unity and peace. The word is therefore taken up again by the prophets to designate one of the forms of *oppression* to which Israel is subjected by its enemies. Habakkuk is surprised: he had thought that the Babylonians were called to re-establish justice (Hab 1.12, *mispath*), but it is exactly the opposite, *hamas*, which they bring (Hab 1.9). In fact, the Babylonians make their own justice (Hab 1.7), and their own might is their god (Hab 1.11); they gather the captives like sand (Hab 1.9), and they kill systematically, without pity (Hab 1.17). *Hamas*, then, is power and might exercise indiscriminately without regard for justice or for the sanctity of human life. Both the exilic and post-exilic prophetic writings describe as *hamas* the war inflicted on Israel (Jer 51.35; Ez 7.11; Joel 4.19; Isa 60.18). Thus these prophets wanted to show that the war undergone by Israel was not a veritable combat, but rather a large-scale repetition of the murder committed by Abimelech (Judg 9). There is nothing noble or heroic in this war. The Babylonian order is nothing but violence and destruction, spoliation and oppression. This war is purely arbitrary, the disruption of the cosmic order, the substitution of might and oppression for the justice and peace of God.

Exploitation

This second form of *hamas* can be divided into two: exploitation by means of robbery, and exploitation by means of local or international commerce. ' "They do not know how to do right" says the Lord, "those who

store up *violence* and *robbery* in their strongholds" '
(Amos 3.10).

Violence and robbery refer here to the goods extorted
from the poor and stored up in the palaces of the rich.
Amos reserves the word *hamas* to describe the *internal
situation of the country,* that of a social 'class' disadvan-
taged by the development of the country. Amos is the
first to use *hamas* on the social level. About a century
later Zephaniah stigmatizes 'those who fill their master's
house with *violence* and *fraud*' (Zeph 1.9). This is usually interpreted as referring to the robberies committed by
'those who are near the throne' (Zeph 1.9 JB) in the
period 640–633 BC. Thus, no matter what means are
used, the poor are exploited and suffer violence; and the
prophet condemns this high administration accordingly:
'The officials within her are roaring lions, her judges are
evening wolves that leave nothing till the morning'
(Zeph 3.3).

Commercial exploitation happens both on the local
and the international level. The first is referred to when
Micah writes, 'Your rich men are full of *violence*; Your
inhabitants speak lies, and their tongue is deceitful in
their mouth' (Mic 6.12). The whole passage, Mic 6.9–12,
is addressed to the city and seems to presuppose the
existence of business people who exploit the small farmers by buying their harvests at low prices and with
tampered scales, and then reselling the product, sometimes even to the producer himself, at an exorbitant
profit. *Hamas* here is parallel with lies and deceit.
Moreover, the reference to false measures and tampered scales implies that *hamas* is an irregularity towards
the weak who cannot defend themselves.

International commerce seems to be in the mind of
Ezekiel when he writes, 'In the abundance of your trade

you were filled with *violence*, and you sinned' (Ezek 28.16a). This verse summarizes the whole of Ezek 27, which describes a profitable business venture. But this verse is not a simple denunciation of commercial exploitation. It refers to a *system* which allows people to have access to property by taking unjust advantage of the work of others; and this is on an international scale.

Abuse of the word

The third form of *hamas*, abuse of the word, expresses itself in false testimony and perfidy. In Exek 23.1; Deut 19.16 and Ps 35.11 we find the expression 'Witness of *hamas*', which means 'false witness', but calls attention to the damage thus done to the other. *Hamas* here refers to lies committed in the social, and more particularly in the juridical domain, which allow the powerful to 'legally' rob or eliminate the poor.

Hamas also means treason, betrayal of the given word or the agreement one has concluded, as in the case of repudiation mentioned in Mal 2.16, 'For I hate divorce, says the Lord God of Israel, and covering one's garment with *violence*, says the Lord of hosts. So take heed to yourselves and do not be faithless.' The text considers repudiation an injustice and aggression because it leaves the wife deprived in society.

The three forms of *hamas*, namely, physical violence, exploitation, and abuse of the word, rarely occur separately. In order to better understand the complexity of the concept we will now consider the role the biblical authors give it in society and in the world.

Hamas in society and in the world

Hamas is the work of those who hold power and, therefore, can make use of force: the king, the judges, the rich.

Hamas and the king

According to Ps 72.14 the king must protect the poor from 'violence'. But, as the prophets repeatedly state, not only do the kings – with very few exceptions, such as Josiah (Jer 22.16) – not defend the defenceless, but they themselves commit 'violence' (Zeph 1.8–9; Jer 22.3; Ez 45.7ff.).

Hamas and justice

This aspect of the question is closely related to the previous in so far as the king, even if he did not personally administer justice, was nevertheless considered ultimately responsible for its exercize. '*Hamas*' becomes the cry of distress by the poor who are faced by the false testimony of the powerful. Especially in the Prophets and the Psalms, *hamas* refers not only to reprehensible acts committed in court, but also to acts which divert the entire organization of justice – the institution which should be the most important element in the realization of harmony in society. Therefore, *hamas* not only describes the result of a particular judgement, but also the way in which judgement in general is given. It is very instructive here to read 1 Kings 21, the story of how Ahab and Jezebel had Naboth condemned to death so that they could get hold of his vineyard. Notice that it is the queen who instigates and engineers the whole affair.

Hamas and riches

Hamas is found especially among the 'haves' who want to have more (Amos 3.10; 6.4; Mic 6.12). Ps 73 offers a striking picture of the rich who lack nothing (verse 4): 'Therefore pride is their necklace; *violence* covers them as a garment. Their eyes swell out with fatness . . .' (verses 6–7); 'Always at ease, they increase their riches' (verse 12). *Injustice* and *violence* are like their garment; i.e., they characterize their whole person.

In conclusion, we may say that the Old Testament, especially in the Prophets, offers us *an analysis of sin which shows it in its political dimensions*. Sin is not just individual; it is also essentially common to a 'class', a nation, and ultimately to the world. *Hamas* is the evil that undermines society. It is not simply the isolated acts of evil persons, but a *system* for which the ruling class is especially responsible. The structures and institutions are affected by it, so that they no longer play the part which they are supposed to play in society. This explains the radicalism of the prophetic message.

Hamas, the great social evil

Isa 59 describes how almost immediately after the Babylonian Exile, when there was hardly enough time for the oppressive structures to get reorganized, *hamas* reappears. This means that *hamas* is not just violence, exploitation, or lie, but ultimately the way of life of the 'evil ones', the 'impious'. In the book of Proverbs *hamas* does not refer to a particular action but rather to a general climate which is fatal for the life of the community. It is a mentality which penetrates the whole person, so that one can speak of 'to drink' (Prov 4.17; 26.6) or 'to eat' violence (Prov 13.2). For the Priestly source of the Pentateuch *hamas* is the injustice of a society which is separated from God and has, therefore, no longer any reference point outside itself.[20]

Discussion Questions

1. Who in the Bible are identified as the victims of violence?/the perpetrators of violence?

2. What are the three basic forms of violence described in the Old Testament?

3. What is meant by the expression 'violence and oppression'?

4. How can the abuse of the word be called violence?

6. The Warrior God and Holy War

The Warrior God

Turning to the book of Joshua, we begin by noting that it

cannot be considered a 'primitive' theology of God
and war which later books replace with a God of love.
The book in its completed form is an indispensable
and climactic part of Israel's epic of her formation as a
nation by the great providential acts of God in western
Asia during the second millennium BC. Formally, it
stands at the beginning of the Deuteronomistic history
of the ways of God with Israel in the Promised Land
(Deut – 2 Kings) . . . Theologically, it furnishes tradi-
tional details about how the initial wars of conquest
were won by Joshua. Israel was victorious, not because they were marvelous fighters under a brilliant
general, but because God went before Israel, threw
fear into the heart of the opposition, and wrought the
victory for his own purposes . . . The victories in the
Conquest were 'not by your sword or by your bow, but
I gave you a land on which you had not labored' (Josh
24.12–13). Biblical references to the conquest generally omit all mention of specific battles and human
activity. It is God's deed; he is the sole actor; there are
no human heroes.[21]

This can be found in texts like Amos 2.9; Ps 78.53–55;
80.8–11, etc.

The conquest was God's free gift to people who had been outcasts in Egypt. This is the conviction of all biblical authors. The Bible's most advanced theologizing in later times saw in the Book of Joshua nothing but a very dramatic illustration of the power, grace, and justice of God. But one should here take into account the institution of holy war, which will be considered in the second part of this chapter.

> God the Warrior is the theme that furnishes hopes in time . . . Wars and rumors of wars are a Biblical reality, a present reality. Yet the strong, active power given language in the Warrior-Lord means that there is a force in the universe set against the forces of evil and perversity. Life, then, is a battleground, but the Divine Warrior will not be defeated. Now if one thinks this type of language is too strong, let him only remember that God the Warrior is simply the reverse of God the Lover or of God the Redeemer. The seeking love of God is only one side of the Suzerain's activity, because, to change the figure, divine love is a two-edged sword. It is power in action in a sinful world, and redemption is disturbing, painful, resisted.[22]

The terror and dread of the enemy before Israel is repeatedly described as one of the works of God the Warrior in holy war. The use of mythic language in describing the Exodus and the Conquest suggests that the re-enactment of these events was probably central to early Israelite worship. Among the features involved in the worship was the celebration of God's leading his people into the land.

While the Divine Warrior as Giver of the land was still celebrated, the new theology of monarchy brought new dimensions to the warrior-theology. The cultus in Jerusalem now celebrated not only the Divine Warrior's past deeds of conquest, but his warfare against the enemies of David and his dynasty until the whole world acknowledged the sovereignty of God and of his anointed Messiah (see e.g., Ps 2). Stability and permanence are the watchwords of the Jerusalem theology, and they are based upon faith in the Divine Warrior to subdue enemies.

Isa 52.7–12 is a proclamation of God's kingship and its effects upon his victorious return to Zion. The thought is that of a second Exodus and Conquest. As the Divine Warrior brought freedom and rest in those first glorious events, so he will do again to the scattered people.

In the 'last days' of apocalyptic expectation, a central feature was the final battle against the forces of evil. In that day 'the Lord will become king over the whole earth' (Zech 14.9).

Holy war

From the beginning of history war has often been conducted in a religious atmosphere and for religious purposes; but there is nothing that we know in the ancient world which corresponds to the Israelite holy war.

The holy war appears both in the narratives of the Old Testament and in laws governing it.

The *laws* of war are found in Deuteronomy 20. War against a distant people is to be preceded by an invitation to surrender and accept forced labour; if the invitation is refused, all adult males are to be killed and the women and children enslaved. The peoples of Canaan, however, are to be killed totally; even their livestock is to be slaughtered, and no booty is to be taken.

Examples of the holy war in the *narratives* are found in the book of Joshua. The principle of total extermination is applied at Jericho (Joshua 6), Ai (Joshua 7), the cities of southern Canaan (Joshua 10), and of northern Canaan (Joshua 11). Eastern Palestine was dealt with in the same way (Num 21). In 1 Sam 15, Saul is deposed from the monarchy by Samuel because in the war against the Amalekites he spared the king of the Amalekites and took booty.

The extermination of captives and livestock is called in most English Bibles the 'ban'. The Hebrew word *herem* really means 'to consecrate', 'to dedicate to the deity'. Persons, livestock and other booty (which was destroyed) were consecrated by being removed from human usage. The 'ban' was thus a prohibition against the ordinary profits of war. One may think of it as an effort to raise the moral level of war, which in the ancient world was a candid act of banditry and piracy aimed at plunder.

A number of scholars think that the laws of war in Deuteronomy are derived from traditions like those in the book of Joshua. They are artificial reconstructions which never existed as practical rules of conduct. The Israelites practised war as their neighbours did; war was generally a secular activity. Scholars also think that the narratives of the holy war are also quite imaginative. They do not take the book of Joshua as a historical narrative of the Israelite conquest. In fact, a number of them think that the Israelite conquest of Palestine was a non-event. The narrative is an imaginative reconstruction formed from local memories and filled out with theological reflection.

This suggests that the episodes which are most appalling never occurred and that the laws existed in a vacuum.

But both in the laws and in the narratives, the ban is proposed as a moral ideal. God himself defeats the enemies; the Israelites are no more than executioners. The book of Joshua presents a land of Canaan in which all inhabitants have been killed, so that there is no one left to claim the land or to oppose the Israelites' possession of it. This is the way in which the finished narrative thought of God as acting, or the way in which the Israelites thought God should have acted.

Gerhard von Rad reconstructed a pattern of holy war behaviour which is widely accepted by scholars. The first action was the consultation of the deity. If a favourable answer was given, the war was proclaimed by the blast of trumpets and the war cry, assuring that Yahweh granted victory. The response to the proclamation was voluntary. The volunteers were consecrated to the service, making the war a cultic act.

The leader of the holy war was chosen because he was manifestly seized by the Spirit of Yahweh, which enabled him to perform heroic feats beyond his normal powers and expectations. The numbers of volunteers were unimportant, for Yahweh was the champion who defeated the enemy. His weapons were nature, as in the storm which mired the Canaanite chariots in Judges 5, and psychology, inspiring a mindless terror in the enemy which drove them to flight in panic (1 Sam 14.15; Joshua 10.10).

The holy war was fought to acquire or to defend the land of promise. The war of Saul against the Philistines (1 Sam 13–14) has elements of the holy war and was clearly fought to defend the land of promise. Similar things can be said about the wars in 1 Sam 7 and 15. There is no sure trace of holy war after David. The wars of David and his successors seem to be quite secular –

wars of conquest or of defence. Moreover, the armies of the kings of Israel and Judea were formed around a corps of professional mercenaries.

The wars of the Maccabees, which were fought in defence of the religion and of the land, were quite rational (insofar as an activity which is essentially immoral can be called rational!).

The holy war is not the only evaluation of war in the Old Testament. Most of the Israelite prophets said something about the wars of Israel and Judah in the eighth and seventh centuries, which were wars of defence against aggression. If military resistance was ever justified against anybody, it was justified against Assyria, and its political heir, Babylonia. Yet Amos, Hosea, Isaiah, Micah and Jeremiah say that the military resistance against Assyria and Babylon is morally wrong; it is offensive to Yahweh. These prophets invert the holy war: Yahweh fights with Assyria and Babylon, and their victory over Israel and Judah is assured. Israel and Judah are so corrupt that God cannot be on their side.

This shows clearly that there is a need to trace a progression in biblical theology and morality. If anything seems to stand at opposite poles, it is the ethic of holy war and the teaching of Jesus on non-violence. But one should speak of 'teaching' with some diffidence; what Jesus said really cannot be condensed or synthesized into a set of ethical rules. If his sayings are turned into rules, the rules contradict each other! They rather communicate an ethos, a spirit, which treats each situation as unique, yet itself remains the same.

Outside the scene of the cleansing of the temple (see Chapter 8), in which the 'violence' is symbolic rather than real, Jesus neither accomplished anything through violence nor recommended that violence be used for any objective, *however noble*. As his words and actions have come down to us, it seems safe to say that if Jesus taught anything, he taught people how to die, not how to kill.[23]

Discussion Questions

1. In what sense and in what context does the Old Testament present God as a Warrior?

2. What does the Bible say about war/holy war?

7. The World in which Christianity was Born

General conditions

The first century A D in which Jesus was born and the early Church developed, was one of the most turbulent centuries in Jewish history.

When Alexander the Great died in 323 B C, Palestine was first under the rule of the Egyptians (323–200 B C), and then of the Syrians (200–142 B C). Then Jewish nationalists secured independence for some seventy years (142–63 B C) until Pompey conquered Palestine for the Roman Empire in 63 B C. From 37 until 4 B C Herod the Great was puppet-king of the Jewish people under the auspices of Rome. Although the Romans did bring some benefits with them, they also brought much violence and devastation. Herod's rule in particular was one of terror, opposed by revolutionaries who favoured the Hasmonean house (descendants of Judas Maccabeus). These revolutionaries waged continual guerrilla warfare against Herod and the Romans, the chief centres of unrest being the royal agricultural estates, where tensions existed between tenants and landlords.[24]

Other factors

Beside the general conditions mentioned above, there were many other causes of unrest in first-century Palestine.

The occupation by foreign troops led to a new social class of foreign colonists, as well as the destruction of forests and loss of other prime materials. Other effects of foreign occupation were heavy taxation and confiscation of land, resulting in increased unemployment which in turn drove many people into the hands of moneylenders. This was aggravated by anti-clericalism and the rift between the aristocratic Sadducean chief priests and the poorer country priests.

A result of these social and economic conditions was the appearance of banditry, often accompanied by violence. Social bandits were the Robin Hoods of the ancient world, and were somehow a symbol of hope for the people. It was from among them that the movement of the Zealots arose between AD 66 and 68 (i.e., thirty to forty years *after* Jesus' death!).

Religious zeal, sometimes developing into fanaticism and terrorism, was common from the time of the Maccabees (175 BC) until the first century AD. Some of the first-century religious revolutionaries did not hestitate to kill even their own friends and relatives. They upheld the concept of holy war, and the Messiah as warrior often appears in the non-biblical Jewish literature. Between AD 36–70 we have evidence of no less than seven revolutionary prophets and messianic pretenders who wanted to overthrow the foreign power and re-establish a theocracy.

Another factor contributing to the unrest was the misconduct of Roman officials, especially from AD 50 on (i.e., some twenty years after Jesus' death). Initial attempts at nonviolent resistance, e.g., in Caesarea around AD 50, gave way to an all-out war in AD 66–74.

Some of the more violent expressions of resistance came from Jewish revolutionary factions, like the *Sicarii* ('dagger-bearers') who staged an attack on the high priest and the upper class in A D 66. The *Zealots*, who appeared as a recognizable faction in A D 67–68, had some initial success, but their terrorism cost them popular support.

As mentioned above, a major cause of Jewish discontent was the Roman system of taxation. According to Luke's chronology, Jesus' birth coincided with an important rebellion against Roman taxation by Judas the Galilean, called 'king' by his followers. Taxation was also one of the major causes of the Roman-Jewish war from A D 66 to 74. When Pompey conquered Palestine in 63 B C he required the Jews to pay tribute. In 57 B C the Jewish people were divided into five districts for the purpose of tax collection. This involved the nomination of Roman 'publicans' – public servants who collected taxes from towns and communities – creating one more alien and unjust practice the people had to cope with. In 6 B C Judea was incorporated into the Empire as a province, and the legate Quirinius took a census of the people to levy taxes according to the Roman practice. This led to the revolt of Judas the Galilean who, after the death of Herod, seized the royal palace and the armory at Sepphoris in Galilee. Tax exemption and political autonomy were closely related.

Finally, in addition to enmity against Rome, there was hostility between Jews and Samaritans, whose territory extended over about a third of Palestine. After the death of Solomon in 931 B C, the Hebrew kingdom had been divided into two, Judah in the south and Israel in the north. Israel, and its capital Samaria, was subjugated by the Assyrians in 721 B C – an event which led to syncretism in culture and religion. After Judah in its turn had been conquered by the Babylonians (in 587 B C), and after the Jews had begun to return from exile, the Samaritans sabotaged the rebuilding of the temple in Jerusalem. Under Alexander the Great the Samaritans built their own temple on Mount Gerizim, but Hyrcanus the Jewish leader (135–104 BC) besieged and destroyed both Samaria and its temple. In 37 BC the Samaritans helped Herod the Great to conquer Jerusalem, and in the first centuries BC and AD the Samaritans were openly pro-Roman. No wonder the two groups hated each other.[25]

Discussion Questions

1. What were the main factors which determined the socio-economic and political situation in Palestine and the Roman empire in Jesus' time?

2. When did the revolutionaries known as the Zealots enter the scene as an organized group?

8.   Violence in the Gospels and Acts

The last sentences of Chapter 6 lead unavoidably to
Jesus and what he may have said and done concerning
violence or nonviolence. One should remember, however, that in the Gospels we are not *immediately* in touch
with Jesus' very own words. The teaching of Jesus has
come down to us through three stages of tradition: first,
Jesus during his ministry in Palestine, then the early
Christian communities from Jesus' death and resurrection until the writing of the Gospels, and finally the
evangelists who wrote the Gospels. When we open our
Bible we are in touch with the third stage. First of all,
then, we have to study what the four evangelists (and the
other New Testament writers) stated. So, we turn here
to a number of texts which have been repeatedly cited in
connection with violence and nonviolence.

'Rob no-one with violence' (Lk 3.14)

This statement is found in Luke's presentation of the
ministry of John the Baptist (Lk 3.1–20), consisting in a
historical presentation of John (Lk 3.1–6), John's call to
conversion (Lk 3.7–9 parallel to Mt 3.7–10), ethical
teaching by John found in Luke only (Lk 3.10–14),
announcement of the Messiah (Lk 3.15–17), and
historical conclusion: the murder of John by Herod
(Lk 3.18–20).

   As indicated above, the first part of John's preaching

in Lk 3.7–9 is identical with Mt 3.7–10 and, therefore, derived from an earlier source. But at once Luke goes out of his way to include the pertinent question, 'What then shall we do?' (Lk 3.10, 12, 14). Apparently, Luke was not satisfied with a general treatment of 'repentance and conversion'. Therefore, in 3.10–14, found in Luke only, the evangelist tackles the question of the *praxis* of conversion. To the multitudes' question John the Baptist, and therefore Luke, answers: sharing! In a world of stark contrasts between rich and poor, powerful and powerless, there cannot be any serious talk about 'conversion' without genuine attempts to *do* (four times in five verses!) something about the existing differences. But even this is not considered sufficient, and Luke singles out two groups for special mention: tax collectors and soldiers. It is already very interesting to see which two groups Luke singles out, but the observation becomes even more challenging if we do not consider them as *two* groups but as *one*: tax collectors accompanied by soldiers!

The tax collectors (i.e., Jews responsible for collecting taxes from various areas in Palestine for the Romans and Herod) are told not to resort to extortion – which, as we have seen, the Old Testament regards as institutionalized violence. The soldiers – not Roman soldiers but Jews enlisted in the service of Herod Antipas – are told not to extort money by violence or to intimidate people, but to be satisfied with their rations or provisions (rather than 'wages').

So, at the beginning of his Gospel, Luke goes out of his way to pinpoint one of the most oppressive realities in the Graeco-Roman world, namely an extremely heavy tax system maintained with the backing of military power.

The ax comes down on the system. Collect no more than is appointed you. These simple words cut through the roots of graft, the pay-off, the kick-back, the torn-up ticket – all the tentacles that reach out to destroy the health and substance, the moral fiber and ethical backbone of an individual and his nation . . . The appearance of soldiers in the narrative next to tax collectors suggests that military force, combined with oppressive systems, comes under special indictment.[26]

Concluding, we may say that Luke points an accusing finger at *institutionalized violence*, very much as the Prophets did in the Old Testament.

'Inside you are all full of extortion' (Lk 11.39; Mt 23.25)

We are dealing here with a saying which occurs in a slightly different form in Matthew and Luke:

Matthew 23.25	Lk 11.39
Woe to you, scribes and Pharisees, hypocrites! for you cleanse the outside of the cup and of the plate, but inside they are full of extortion and rapacity.	Now you Pharisees cleanse the outside of the cup and of the dish, but inside you are full of extortion and wickedness.

The meaning of Mt 23.25 is that the cups and plates are full *because* of extortion and rapacity, that is, the food and drink were acquired by avarice and injustice, which no amount of cultic washing could cleanse. These Pharisees pretended to be pure while, in fact, being full of robbery and wickedness. Again we are dealing with a kind of *institutionalized* violence. By their behaviour, the Pharisees also failed in their responsibility to make clear the will of God. They focused on the cleansing of utensils (and other practices) while God's will, expressed in the Law, was really concerned with *people* and the development of moral character. Thus they did violence to the people on two counts: by their extortion and injustice, but also by denying them a true understanding of God's will.[27]

The meaning of Lk 11.39 depends on whether 'you' (in Greek 'of you') is connected with 'inside' or with 'extortion and wickedness'. The former interpretation implies that the application is inserted into the metaphor: the Pharisees may be ritually clean externally, but their hearts are filled with greed. If the latter interpretation is accepted, the point is that the cups and dishes used by the Pharisees are full of the proceeds of their rapacity which is practically the same as what is said in Mt 23.25.[28]

Entering the Kingdom violently (Lk 16.16; Mt 11.12)

Here again we are dealing with a saying which appears in different forms in Matthew and Luke:

Mt 11.12–13	Lk 16.16
From the days of John the Baptist until now the kingdom of heaven has suffered violence, and men of violence take it by force. For all the prophets and the law prophesied until John.	The law and the prophets were until John; since then the good news of the kingdom of God is preached, and every one enters it —violently.

There is no way of telling which evangelist has preserved either the *original* order of these sayings (ie, the first stage of the Gospel tradition) or the order in the Q-source (the second stage of the Gospel tradition) but most commentators favour the order of Luke. Lk 16.16 is an important element in Lucan theology, and especially in Luke's view of three periods of salvation history: (1) the Old Testament ('until John'), (2) the time of Jesus ('since then . . . every one enters it violently'), and (3) the Church (Acts of the Apostles).

An analysis of the Matthean and Lucan *forms* of the saying leads to an original Q-saying which was transmitted approximately as follows:

> 'The law and the prophets were until John; since then the kingdom of god has suffered violence (*biazetai*), and every one enters it violently (*biazetai*).'

The verb *biazein* means 'to force', but it is most frequently used in the middle voice, 'make use of force', either in a positive sense ('try hard') or in a negative, hostile sense ('use force on/against'). The positive sense has been preferred by many scholars, but the problem has always been to explain how that sense would be true of 'every one'. Other commentators have preferred the negative sense, 'use violence against it'. But who is meant by 'every one'? The second group seem to intend to make Luke say what Mt 11.12 says. In the Matthean context, the threefold mention of violence ('violence', 'of violence', and 'by force') refers to what happened to John the Baptist, who in Matthew's version is a preacher of the Kingdom. But such a meaning does not suit the Lucan context, or the Gospel as a whole. In Luke the saying is probably to be understood as meaning: 'the message of the kingdom of God is still being preached and every one is pressed to enter it'; literally, 'every one is forced into it' (i.e., with a demanding, urgent invitation from the kingdom-preacher, who in Luke is not John the Baptist, but Jesus himself.)[29] If this interpretation is right, then 'every one' may mean 'not only the righteous, but *every one*, including publicans and sinners'.

The saying, then, in its Lucan form does not contain a reference to violence as such; whereas the Matthean version refers to the *institutionalized violence* of which John the Baptist was the victim at the hands of Herod, the puppet-king.

'If anyone strikes you on the (right) cheek' (Mt 5.39; Lk 6.29)

This statement is part of the Sermon on the Mount (Mt 5.1—7.29) the Lucan parallel being found in the Sermon on the Plain (Lk 6.20—49).

> The more proximate context is the units Mt 5.38–48 and Lk 6.27–36. In Luke this unity is underlined by the opening admonition to 'love your enemies' in 6.27 and its closing repetition, 'love your enemies' in 6.35a. Matthew has modified his source much more radically in order to fit it into his set of six antitheses in 5.21–26 (murder), 27–30 (adultery), 31–32 (divorce), 33–37 (oaths), 38–42 (revenge), and 43–48 (hate) . . . The cheek saying, therefore, now appears in the fifth of Matthew's six antitheses, but within the more general frames of 'love your enemies' in Luke. Or, in other words, the aphorism is *within* the 'love your enemies' command in Luke 6.27b–35a but comes *before* the sixth antithesis on hating/loving your enemies in Mt 5.43–48.[30]

Mt 5.39–42	Lk 6.29–30
But I say to you, Do not resist one who is evil.	
But if anyone strikes you on the right cheek, turn to him the other also;	To him who strikes you on the cheek, offer the other also;
and if anyone would sue you and take your coat, let him have your cloak as well;	and from him who takes away your cloak, do not withhold your coat as well.
and if anyone forces you to go one mile, go with him two miles.	
Give to him who begs from you, and do not refuse him who would borrow from you.	Give to everyone who begs from you; and from him who takes away your goods do not ask them again.

Striking somebody on the *right* cheek was considered especially contemptuous, since it can be done only with the back of the hand; it was a double insult liable to double damages. But it is said here that the disciple should turn the other cheek and suffer the most hurting insult, rather than answer it with retaliation, denunciation or lawsuits. Thus Jesus does not order us simply to turn the other cheek (he did not do so himself during his trial), but he enjoins us very seriously to set out resolutely on the road of banning from our hearts all feelings and intentions of revenge and retaliation. This is a *goal*-commandment rather than a law, a direction rather than a directive.

The same goes for giving one's cloak or coat, and going two miles instead of one. The first should be understood against the background of Ex 22.26–27 and Deut 24.12–13, where a poor man's cloak, given in pawn or pledge, must be returned before nightfall, because the cloak was also the poor man's covering for the night, one of the basic necessities of life. Going one mile presumably refers to the hated conscripted service demanded (as in the case of Simon of Cyrene in Mt 27.32) by the imperial invaders.

In Matthew, the whole paragraph is presented under the heading, 'Do not resist one who is evil.' Does Mt 5.39 constitute a manifesto for pacifism and announce a principle of not resisting evil?

What then does Matthew 5.39 mean? It means two very radical things: (1) that one should not resist evil persons by exacting equal damages for injury suffered (i.e., an eye for an eye); and (2) that one should not respond to an evil person by placing him in the category of enemy. Indeed, one should love one's enemy, even at great personal cost. The good of the other person, not one's own needs or rights, are decisive. Jesus' command not to resist evil must be understood in the light of the preceding verse. To exact an eye for an eye was the accepted norm. But Jesus rejected that way of dealing with evil persons. One should not resist evil that way. The Greek preposition *anti* (which means 'opposite' or 'instead of') or 'in place of' appears in both verses. It appears in the phrase 'an eye for (*anti*) an eye and a tooth for (*anti*) a tooth.' Then it appears in the verb 'resist' (*antistenai*). Literally *antistenai* means 'to stand opposite' or 'to place against'. The repetition of the preposition in both verses suggests that one is not to place oneself against the evil person in the way indicated in verse 38, which was the normally accepted way – i.e., by exacting equal damages for injury suffered. In fact, one is to respond to evil by refusing to place the person who inflicts evil in the category of an enemy to be hated or injured. Instead of categorizing the person who harms one as an enemy, one is to love him . . . One should respond with that kind of astonishing, unexpected love for the evil person even when he strikes one's right cheek with the back of his hand, which was considered the most insulting of all physical blows. *But that does not mean that we cannot offer any form of resistance to the evil person.* That would contradict Jesus' own rebuke of the soldier who struck him on the cheek. Rather it means that Jesus' kind of resistance to evil will be of the sort that refuses to exact equal damages for injury suffered, that refuses to consider anyone an enemy no matter how outrageous his offense and therefore that continues to demonstrate active aggressive love controlled by the need of the evil person. Thus Jesus' saying is compatible with the use of economic, legal, or political power to oppose evil as long as love for the oppressor as well as the oppressed is both the means and the end.[31]

But all this is an ideal, a goal, an orientation, a direction; not a directive, not a law to be kept in a literal sense, here and now. Jesus wants us resolutely to set out in this direction, discerning *as a community* as well as individuals what should be our creative response to a given conflict situation. The goal of this demand, as of the whole Sermon on the Mount, is nothing less than unlimited and unconditional concern for the well-being of our fellow-person. But in the process we, as a community and as individuals, will often fail to meet that goal, and we may find that acts of violence will happen on the road to that goal. None of these, however, are decisive, if we consider our lives as a process, as a journey towards our communal goal, the kingdom of God. For God's kingdom is *becoming*, not finished, and its ethic, therefore, is also a process of dynamic growth, not a once-and-for-all established set of immutable demands.

Violence and persecution (Lk 13.1ff., 31–33)

> There were some present at that very time who told
> him of the Galileans whose blood Pilate had mingled
> with their sacrifices (Lk 13.1).

The text gives the impression of a report about something that has recently happened. Presumably Pilate's
soldiers had cut down a number of people while they
were slaughtering sacrificial animals, possibly Paschal
lambs. Luke's presentation of Pilate in this story is in
keeping with Josephus' description of Pilate as a brutal
person.

Another example of political brutality is found in the
person of Herod:

> At that very hour some Pharisees came, and said to
> him, 'Get away from here, for Herod wants to kill
> you.' And he said to them, 'Go and tell that fox . . .'
> (Lk 13.31–33).

Herod had already imprisoned and beheaded John
the Baptist (Lk 3.19–20; 9.9a), and Jesus was aware of
this . . . The Pharisees who report this desire of
Herod to kill Jesus now urge him to move on. Jesus'
uncompromising reply makes use of an unflattering
term about the tetrarch of Galilee, the holder of
political power, summing up his estimate of Herod's
character and expressing his defiance of Herod's pre-
tensions. Though Jesus does not trust Herod, he uses
the warning to make a fundamental declaration about
his own ministry and journey. He will go on teaching
and freeing human beings until he reaches his 'goal' or
destiny (verse 32). His ministry has no political con-
notations (recall 4.43), and he will continue, not out of
fear of Herod, a political authority, but because he

must – because he is subject to another authority.[32]

The warning of the Pharisees points to the *status quo* which Jesus is disturbing. Herod shows the characteristics of petty people who are frightened by anyone who raises questions or rocks the boat. Jesus is on his way to Jerusalem, but not in order to escape from Herod. There is a clear intimation here that Jesus is to suffer a prophet's death.

'It is expedient that one man should die' (Jn 11.50)

So the chief priests and the Pharisees gathered the council, and said, 'What are we to do? For this man performs many signs. If we let him go on thus, every one will believe in him, and the Romans will come and destroy both our [holy] place and our nation.' But one of them, Caiaphas, who was high priest that year, said to them, 'You know nothing at all; you do not understand that it is expedient for you that one man should die for the people, and that the whole nation should not perish . . .' (Jn 11.47–50).

The theme of the scene, the contrast between the 'one' and the 'whole nation', is set up; it is developed as the expression of political anxiety in verse 48 and it reaches its climax in the decisive saying of Caiaphas the high priest, which is said to be prophetic. In verse 49 this is introduced and in verse 50 it is formulated. In verse 51 it is established as prophecy, but in verse 52 it receives comment along the lines of a particularly important Johannine theological statement . . . Verse 53 contains the decision of the Sanhedrin, while verse 54 describes evasive action on Jesus' part. Verse 57 reports the decree of the Sanhedrin stating the responsibility of anyone who knows where Jesus may be staying to pass on the information so that he can be arrested. In other words, an arrest warrant is issued . . . The influence of Jesus on the people is thus seen by the members of the Sanhedrin as a danger. The activity of Jesus reinforces the gap between the people and the Sanhedrin . . . Perplexity and fear move Caiaphas to his decisive intervention.[33]

The Supreme Court of the Jewish people, embodying the interests of the Jewish establishment, were becoming scared of Jesus' growing influence. But apparently the body was not able accurately to assess the situation. Caiaphas, their president, finally stated that it was 'expedient for the people' (i.e., for those who claim to 'represent the people') that one man should be sacrificed. In present-day language he was saying that 'it is necessary for national security' – or 'for the interests of the party', as the case may be – that one man be sacrificed. John also perceptively identified the deeper cause of so much brutality and violence perpetrated by people in power, namely *fear* for one's position. (The Greek text has 'our place' instead of 'our holy place', and may well be referring to the position of the Sanhedrin.) 'The Jews have their own motive for their course of action: self-preservation. How can Pilate be persuaded? Eventually, only by an appeal to the same motive (19.12).'[34] Initially Pilate did not seem too eager to go along with the chief priests and their plans, but he eventually ceded to their pressure, when they told him, 'If you release this man, you are not Caesar's friend' (Jn 19.12). Not to be the friend of Caesar (or the king, or the president, or the chairman) is to jeopardize your job. So the chief priests and Pilate conspired to preserve their positions of power. And, as we can see in Jn 11.57, the Sanhedrin did not hesitate to make use of informers to acheive their goal.

The cleansing of the temple (Mk 11.15–19; Mt 21.12–13; Lk 19.45–48; Jn 2.13–17)

> And he entered the temple and began to drive out those who sold and those who bought in the temple, and he overturned the tables of the money-changers and the seats of those who sold pigeons; and he did not allow any one to carry anything through the temple (Mk 11.15–16).

Matthew does not have the last item; Luke simply states: 'And he entered the temple and began to drive out those who sold' (Lk 19.45).

> In the temple he found those who were selling oxen and sheep and pigeons, and the money-changers at their business. And making a whip of cords, he drove them all, with the sheep and oxen, out of the temple; and he poured out the coins of the money-changers and overturned their tables. And he told those who sold the pigeons, 'Take these things away . . .' (Jn 2.14–16).

This scene has been blown up by some writers into a full-fledged revolution! Sound scholarship, however, has never accepted this thesis.

> Its importance should not be exaggerated, but it has very great consequences for Jesus . . . Critics who, like Robert Eisler and S.G.F. Brandon, turn this incident in the Temple into a large-scale military operation, are obliged to assume that Jesus acted as

the leader of a secret army, or that he held 'Zealot'
convictions which are incompatible with all the rest of
the gospel tradition. Since in any case the narrative of
the driving out of the merchants from the Temple is a
very slight basis for the reconstruction of a pitched
battle, it is difficult to find grounds for a thesis of this
kind . . . [But] Jesus' action towards the merchants, a
very rapid action with no further consequences, may
have taken on the dimensions of a great event in
Jewish opinion.[35]

It is true that authors like Robert Eisler (1930), Joel
Carmichael in *The Death of Jesus* (1963), and S.G.F.
Brandon in *Jesus and the Zealots* (1967), as well as
Hans-Werner Bartsch, stated that the temple-cleansing
was an action with political character. According to
Bartsch it signified 'not only an end to the privileged
status of the priesthood but also a threat to the Roman
occupational rule . . . If his action was no bluff, then
Jesus was either a Zealot or else became one.' Furthermore, 'As a revolutionary he belonged to them even
though his revolution looked different than the one
attempted by the Zealots.' But many of the best biblical
scholars have opposed this interpretation on solid
grounds. For example, the well-known biblical scholar
and historian Martin Hengel writes:

In the so-called temple-cleansing we have,
apparently, a prophetic demonstration or, one could
also say, provocation, in which it was not a matter of
driving out all those who sold and the money-
changers . . . We are dealing, rather, with a demon-
strative condemnation of their trade, a condemnation
which was directed at the same time against the ruling
temple aristocracy, which derived profit from it. It

may also be assumed here that the word, not the action, stood at the center – such an isolated action would have been meaningless by itself.[36]

To that we may add that, as far as Jesus' connections with the Zealots are concerned, we showed in the previous chapter that the Zealots emerged as an organized movement only well after Jesus' death. So many of the claims of a tie-up between Jesus and the Zealots fall into the trap of anachronism.

The so-called 'cleansing' of the Temple was not a *coup* or take-over of the Temple as a first step towards the conquering of Jerusalem, as some authors have maintained . . . Jesus took action in the vast courtyard of the Gentiles and not in the Holy Place where the sacrifices were offered and he took action because of the traders and money-changers. In other words, his concern, as we might well expect from what we have seen so far, was not to gain power or to purify ritual. His concern was *the abuse of money and trade* . . . His compassion for the poor and the oppressed overflowed once more into indignation and anger . . . Some authors have entertained the bizarre idea that Jesus and his disciples engaged the Temple police and perhaps even the Roman garrison in battle and that for a while Jesus held out against them and maintained his control of the Temple. This is historically impossible not only because it does not accord with what Jesus had said and done up till then nor with subsequent events but also because it would certainly have been recorded in the annals of the Jewish historian Josephus as an event of considerable political and military importance.[37]

We would say that the temple-cleansing was *more than* just an effort to remove certain abuses in the temple, but that Jesus had a real case against the temple. His action of cleansing the temple was a *prophetic protest* and a *sign* that the temple in its present setting had lost its relevance and would soon disappear. But it was *not* a violent occupation of the temple. It cannot be interpreted as evidence that Jesus favoured or condoned violence to establish the Kingdom.

The two swords (Lk 22.35–38)

> And he said to them, 'When I sent you out with no purse or bag or sandals, did you lack anything?' They said, 'Nothing'. He said to them, 'But now, let him who has a purse take it, and likewise a bag. And let him who has no sword sell his mantle and buy one. For I tell you that this scripture must be fulfilled in me, "And he was reckoned with transgressors"; for what is written about me has its fulfilment.' And they said, 'Look, Lord, here are two swords.' And he said to them, 'It is enough.' (Lk 22.35–38).

This passage is found in Luke only. It belongs to the discourse which in Luke immediately follows the institution of the Eucharist which comprises four units:

(1) verses 21–23, the prophecy about the betrayal of Jesus by Judas, which occurs before the supper in Mark and Matthew, but afterwards in Luke;

(2) verses 24–30, the dispute about greatness among the twelve;

(3) verses 31–34, the prediction that Satan will sift Peter;

(4) verses 35–38, the two-swords passage.

'When we read all these four . . . a climax is reached on the prophetic disclosures of the last unit of material, the verses about the sword.'[38] Moreover, Lk 22.35–38 constitute the last words of Jesus during the last supper and must, therefore, be very important to Luke.

A confusing number of interpretations have been given to this passage. It has been seen by some as insistent appeal to the disciples to buy swords at all costs, and by others as an attempt to convert violent revolutionaries! It has been considered both as completely symbolic and as altogether realistic, as situated in Jesus' ministry before Easter as well as in the early Church after Easter.[39]

The burning question is, of course, what does Jesus mean by his command to purchase a sword in verse 36? Is this to be understood literally or is it intended figuratively? The question is further complicated by Jesus' response to the disciples when they actually produce two swords: 'It is enough' (Lk 22.38).

From the time of the Church Fathers all interpretations held today (except for a literal interpretation of the sword which Jesus commanded his disciples to purchase, perhaps for the purpose of self-defence) can already be found. We need not discuss the interpretation initiated by Ambrose who understood the two swords to represent the Law and the Gospel, or the interpretation prevailing in the Middle Ages in which the two swords came to be associated in an allegorical fashion with the power of the Church and the power of the State. At the time of the Reformation, both Luther and Calvin understood the text in a figurative or spiritual sense; whereas later scholarship shows increasing interest in a literal understanding of Jesus' sword-word, relating it to Peter's action in Gethsemane, or to the subsequent persecution of the apostles.

More recently, scholars have been concerned with questions such as: Why was Lk 22.35–38 placed in its present context? When did this arrangement occur? And, Who did the arrangement? In recent literature we can identify at least *six primary proposals* for understanding Jesus' command to purchase a sword.

1.   Firstly, there is the 'charade theory' which understands Jesus as urging the disciples to act out the part of robbers and 'transgressors' (literally, 'lawless') since they are going to be 'reckoned' among such anyway. So Jesus did not mean his disciples to take his instruction literally, and their action in verse 38 (producing two swords) therefore constitutes a misunderstanding. Jesus' words, 'It is enough', are paraphrased by F.W. Danker, 'two swords should make us look sufficiently like brigands'. In other words the irony concerns not the number of the swords, but the whole mentality of the apostles.[40]

2.   The 'prediction theory' says that Jesus was foretelling the disciples' faithless and disobedient reaction in lifting up swords to defend him. The 'transgressors' among whom Jesus is reckoned would therefore be the disciples themselves. 'The use of the sword by the apostles and police affords twin witnesses to "the powers of the darkness" (verse 53).'[41] But there is an obvious difficulty in construing Jesus' words as a prediction. Moreover, by transgressors it is far more likely that Luke has in mind the two criminals between whom Jesus was crucified, rather than the disciples. Furthermore, Jesus' opponents also reckoned him among the lawless by sentencing him to be crucified in the place of Barabbas, an insurgent.

3.   Another proposal is that Jesus ordered his disciples to procure swords because he was afraid of being assas-

sinated. The swords were for his and the disciples'
self-defence during the time of the Passover feast in
Jerusalem. But attributing to Jesus fear for *his own* life
would make it necessary to construe the teaching and
ministry of Jesus in a totally different way from that
recorded in the Gospels (especially in the Sermon on the
Mount). Jesus would ultimately have surrendered to the
temptation to rely on force, giving up his path of suffering and death on practical grounds. This sort of construc-
tion depends on an unusually imaginative insight into
the psychology of Jesus derived from unnamed sources!

4.   Some scholars understand the text as referring to a
'sword for the holy war'. They try to understand Jesus as
a first-century Jew (which is valid), but link him with one
particular strand of Jewish apocalyptic, characterized by
the nationalistic desire to see an independent Jewish
nation, liberated from its oppressors, the Romans. This
liberation was to be the work of God, achieved by the
active participation of his faithful people in his holy war.
In his enthusiasm to prove his point Eisler goes as far as
saying that the apostles showed Jesus *two swords each*![42]
Brandon quotes Lk 22.35–38 again and again as his most
important proof-text, but mere repetition establishes
nothing. He too cannot believe that there were only two
swords.

The question of the relation between Jesus and the
Zealots has been seriously studied. Still, the conclusion
seems inescapable: when Jesus and the Zealots are
closely compared we see mostly a contrast. In what is to
date the fullest treatment of Lk 22.35–38, Bartsch subjects the sword-saying to considerable editing to make it
justify the actions of the Christians in Jerusalem at the
time of the outbreak of the hostilities in AD 66, and
especially during the siege of Jerusalem, in which those

who had nothing (the 'have-nots') took up swords and joined the defence of the city. These conclusions presuppose an ability to go behind the text which is far beyond the real possibilities. This 'interpretation' is also obviously straining for contemporary relevance. In fact, it reminds us of the medieval efforts to use the sword-saying to legitimate Christian participation in warfare.

A.J. Mattill relies heavily for his interpretation on the holy war teaching in the Old Testament and Jewish apocalyptic, especially Ezek 38—39, which provides for him the framework for a whole sequence of events (the 'last things') predicted by Jesus according to Luke's Gospel. But a close comparison highlights the contrasts rather than the similarities.

5.   Another theory is that Jesus was referring to 'a sword for self-defence'. The most thorough modern exponent of this theory is Oscar Cullman,[43] for whom the basic purpose of the sword-saying is to warn the disciples about 'the persecution to which every disciple will be exposed' as he proclaims the gospel. The sword must be understood literally. Lk 22.35–38 reckons with 'eventualities in which, for the sake of the proclamation of the Gospel, defensive sword-bearing may become a necessity for the disciples.'[44] The words 'It is enough' (Lk 22.38) as well as 'No more of this!' (Lk 22.51) intend to limit the scope of self-defence, clearly marking it off from any concept of violent revolt such as the Zealots urged. Other exponents of the self-defence theory understand the passage as indicating that the apostolic mission is characterized as a time of hostility and persecution in contrast to the period of the earlier missionary ventures in Galilee. The primary argument for taking the sword command literally is its close association with the purse, knapsack, sandals, and garment.

But is it so obvious that these 'concrete necessities of life' are to be taken literally? Is Jesus providing the disciples with a 'traveller's checklist' for their next journey? Cullman and others stress the importance of the apostolic mission which must be defended at all costs. But we search Acts in vain to find the disciples using any sort of force or violence to defend either themselves or the gospel.

6.   Finally, there is the 'figurative interpretation'. All commentators are agreed that in verses 35—36 a contrast is being drawn between two periods of time and their corresponding states of affairs. The words 'but now' in verse 36 must be a decisive pivot in time. Before and after this point the epochs have very different characteristics. But the contrast in verses 35–36 should not be absolutized.

In the following paragraphs we will briefly consider three points: (1) the citation of Isa 53.12 in verse 37: 'and was reckoned with transgressors [literally, lawless]' (2) the broader context of Luke-Acts; and (3) the immediate context of Lk 22.35–38.

There is almost universal agreement that the *citation* of Isa 53.12 carries the explanation for the preceding command to purchase a sword, and that it refers to Jesus' death. 'For what is written about me has its fulfilment' (Lk 22.37c RSV), or 'my life is drawing to its end/goal' (Steen), clarifies the significance of the citation. The effect of the citation and the verse as a whole is to link the future experience of the disciples to Jesus' death on the cross. The disciples will share Jesus' rejection by the world at large. But we feel that the nature of the change indicated by 'but now' is not *primarily* that the disciples will be persecuted like Jesus, but that they will now be sent on a mission to preach the gospel 'to the end of the earth' (Acts 1.8), instead of just to 'the lost sheep of Israel'. But what about verse 38? What is the connection with verse 37? It seems to indicate that the disciples react not to the scripture citation (verse 37) but to the preceding word of Jesus about purchasing a sword (verse 36). It should also be noted that the language of the citation of Isa 53.12 in verse 37 has influenced Luke's description of Jesus' death between two evildoers. It is on Golgotha that Isa 53.12 is fulfilled.

As to the *broader context* of Luke-Acts, Lk 22.35–38 seems to contradict the whole tenor of the earlier missionary instructions in Lk 9.3–5 and 10.4–11. This implies that Jesus is not primarily foretelling hostility and opposition but rather recommissioning the disciples to a task of witness which would proceed from the completion of his own mission (see Lk 22.37c); ie, cross, resurrection, ascension, pentecost. Jesus' goal has been reached and the gospel is now to be preached to the nations (Acts 1.8). Neither Lk 10.4, 'carry no purse, no bag, no sandals, and salute no one on the road', nor Lk 22.36 are to be taken literally. They figuratively characterize the two different missions. But how does the mention of the sword add to this characterization of the mission which is occasioned by Jesus' death, resurrection and ascension? As we have seen, it is usually said that it suggests hostility and persecution which will be met in the future. But according to Lk 22.36 the swords are supposed to be in the *disciples*' hands! How can this be understood in the light of the rebuke in Lk 22.49 and the whole tenor of Jesus' teaching which is so clearly non-violent? It may mean that the 'sword' which Jesus brought into the world (see above on Lk 12.51/Mt 10.34) is now placed in the hands of his disciples upon the attainment of his goal. The 'sword' then is the word of the gospel which will cause division between those who accept it and those who do not (compare Hosea 6.5; Rev 1.16; 2.12, 16; 19.15, 21).

Concerning the *immediate context*, it should be stressed that Lk 22.35–38 is embedded in a context, as part of a careful arrangement (see above) designed to communicate a message to the believing community. The sword-saying is inevitably coloured by its position in the narrative of the Lord's Supper and the Passion. The Last Supper is Jesus' gift to his community which will continue to shape its life. The passage immediately preceding Lk 22.35–38 relates Jesus' prayer for Peter whom the Satan will 'shake' (Lk 22.31–34), which prompts some interpreters to relate the 'sword' to the 'Christian's daily battle against temptation, particularly in times of persecution.'[46] This is confirmed by the fact that the following scene in Gethsemane is framed by Jesus' repeated command to the disciples to 'pray that you may not enter into temptation' (Lk 22.40, 45).

Concluding, we would say that the study of the broader and more immediate context leads in two directions. The broader context suggests that the sword refers to the *preaching of the Word of God* and the consequent *division* among people which this creates. In the more immediate context of Luke's narrative of the Lord's Supper and the Passion, the sword-saying cannot be specifically identified, but must be seen in more general terms, along with the purse and knapsack, as referring to the 'spiritual weaponry' (prayer in particular) which the disciples must possess to carry out their missionary task.

Conclusion

The general conclusion to our study of the New

Testament texts must be that at no time in his ministry did Jesus encourage people to use violence to carry out their mission, and that Jesus himself never used violence to fulfil his mission either. The question as to whether violence is to be altogether rejected, or can be accepted in certain situations and under certain conditions by a Christian today, does not solely depend on whether he can pinpoint one or a few texts in which Jesus seems either to reject or to encourage and condone violence. This approach would understand the 'imitation of Jesus' in a kind of carbon-copy way. To decide this issue the total biblical witness must be dealt with in a responsible manner. In other words, one should first try to assess the gospel message as a whole and determine the values Jesus stood for and died for. Next, any persons or communities who find themselves in an extreme situation, in which they can sincerely say that they have exhausted all non-violent means to secure these values, should ask themselves whether they can in conscience engage themselves in a line of action which at a given point may entail the use of violence.

The following should also be noted. Firstly, the question of violence cannot fully be answered in a vacuum or in theory, but only in a concrete crisis situation.

Secondly, violence does not begin and end the moment a person is killed. Violence covers a whole range of actions, and the dividing line between violence and non-violence is not so clear as is sometimes suggested.

Thirdly, one should not talk about violence in an unqualified way; it should be clear what sort of violence one is talking about. Is it, for example, the violence of those in power used to oppress weaker parties, or is it the 'violence' used by the underdog to overthrow an oppressor? As we saw, the Old Testament refers only to the former as violence, and condemns it. However, the New Testament seems to speak of all forms of violence. This last point will be further developed in the final reflection.

Discussion Questions

1. Discuss 'Rob no one with violence' (Lk 3.14).

2. Discuss 'You are full of extortion' (Lk 11.39).

3. What is the meaning of 'entering the kingdom with violence' (Lk 16.16)?

4. Discuss 'If any one strikes you on the right cheek' (Mt 5.39).

5. What does Luke say about Jesus' experience of violence and persecution (Lk 13)?

6. Discuss the statement of Caiaphas: 'It is expedient that one man should die' (Jn 11.50).

7. Was the cleansing of the temple (Mk 11.15–18 and parallels) a real act of violence? Was it part of a nation-wide revolution? What was its real meaning?

8. Did Jesus' words during the Last Supper encourage the disciples to buy swords (Lk 22.35–38)?

9. Which of the six presently most defended explanations of Lk 22.35–38 do you prefer? Why?

10. What does Lk 22.35–38 seem to say when we take into account the broader context of Luke-Acts?

11. What does Lk 22.35–38 seem to say when we focus on the immediate context of Lk 22?

9. Final Reflection

In the Old Testament, peace results from *justice* (right-eousness); to obtain peace, one has to practise justice (Isa 32.17). But in the New Testament, justice itself becomes the problem. The New Testament question is not how to obtain peace but how to obtain justice. Justice is not something we ourselves have, based on the law, but something which is brought about through faith in Christ (Phil 3.9). Peace as *shalom*, the well-being and salvation of all, remains a concern; but now the problem of justice, which is the key to peace, comes to the fore. This New Testament shift in emphasis does not contra-dict the Old Testament, but completes it both in logic and content.

One of the characteristics of *shalom* is that it is conditional: if you do justice, you will have peace. What is conditional is not the connection between justice and peace – that is absolute – but the realization of justice. Israel's choice was not between willing peace and not willing it, but between willing justice or not willing it. The presence or absence of peace was and is the result of a choice. Thus the obstacle to peace was not and is not something external to Israel or to people today. 'God's enemy' was not the opposing army but the possibility, rooted in Israel's heart as in the hearts of people today, of choosing against justice.[47]

In most treatments of peace, considerable space is given to *reconciliation*. (Paul relates the two to each other in 2 Cor 5.) In this connection I would like to refer extensively to *Taking Sides* by Albert Nolan.[48]

To many of us it is pretty obvious that there are some conflicts in which we ought to take sides. But what about the Christian belief in reconciliation, forgiveness and peace? How can you take sides if you love everybody, including your enemies? And how do we account for the widespread belief that in any conflict a Christian should be a peacemaker who avoids taking sides and try to bring about a reconciliation between opposing forces?

This belief rests on a *mistaken understanding of reconciliation*. We have all heard people say: We must be fair, we must listen to both sides. If we could only get people to talk to one another to sort out their misunderstandings and misconceptions of one another the conflict could be resolved. On the face of it this sounds very Christian. It sounds like a genuine concern for fairness and justice. So what is wrong with this argument?

In the first place it makes reconciliation an *absolute principle* that must be applied in *all* cases of conflict. The model or example that it envisages is that of what one might call 'private quarrel' between two people who are being argumentative and not trying to understand one another and whose differences are based upon misunderstandings. *But not all conflicts are like that*. In some conflicts one side is right and the other wrong, one side is being unjust and oppressive and the other is suffering injustice and oppression. In such cases a policy of seeking consensus and not taking sides would be quite wrong. Christians are not supposed to try to reconcile good and evil, justice and injustice; we are supposed to do away with evil, injustice and sin.

The second mistake in this argument is that it assumes that a person can be neutral in all cases of conflict. In fact, neutrality is not always possible, and in cases of conflict due to injustice and oppression neutrality is totally impossible. If we do not take sides with the oppressed, then we are, albeit unintentionally, taking sides with the oppressor. 'Bringing the two sides together' in such cases is actually extremely beneficial to the oppressor, because it enables the status quo to be maintained.

Thirdly, the commonly held view that Christians should always seek harmony and a 'middle way' in every dispute assumes that tension and conflict are worse evils than injustice and oppression. This again is a false supposition based upon a lack of compassion for those who suffer under oppression. Those who are afraid of conflict or confrontation, even when it is non-violent, are usually those who are not convinced of the need for change. Their caution hides an un-Christian pessimism about the future, a lack of hope. Or they use the Christian concern for reconciliation to justify a form of escapism from the realities of injustice and conflict.

So far Nolan. But does not Jesus' clear command, 'Do not resist one who is evil' (Mt 5.39) contradict all this? To quote R.J. Sider:

Does Jesus' command not preclude the use of economic and political power to oppose unjust, evil persons and structures? Some have thought so and argued that Jesus' followers dare not use force of any kind to resist evil. But to interpret Matthew 5.39 in that way is surely to prove too much. If we are to interpret it literally, then we must consistently apply it in a literal fashion in every area . . . Either Matthew 5.39 demands absolute non-resistance toward evil in every area or we dare not interpret it absolutely literally in any area. Numerous actions in the life of Jesus would seem to support the latter alternative. Jesus constantly opposed evil persons in a forthright, vigorous fashion. He unleashed a blistering attack on the Pharisees . . . Nor was Jesus nonresistant when He cleansed the temple! He engaged in aggressive resistance against evil when He marched into the temple, drove the animals out with a whip, dumped the money tables upside down, and denounced the money changers as robbers. If Matthew 5.39 means that all forms of resistance to evil are forbidden, then Jesus contradicted His own teaching. Jesus certainly did not kill the money changers. Indeed, I doubt that He even used His whip on them. But He certainly resisted their evil in a dramatic act of civil disobedience. Or consider Jesus' response when a soldier unjustly struck Him on the cheek at His trial (John 18.19–24). Instead of turning the other cheek and meekly submitting to this injustice, 'He protested! Apparently Jesus thought that protesting police brutality or engaging in civil disobedience in a nonviolent fashion was entirely consistent with His command not to resist one who is evil.[49]

But was not Jesus inspired by the figure of the Suffering Servant in Isaiah? The evangelists say that at his baptism (Mk 1.9–11; Mt 3.13–17; Lk 3.21–22), Jesus understood that it was God's will for him to fulfil his mission as a Servant-Messiah. That is the meaning of the words spoken by the voice from heaven, 'This is my beloved Son [i.e., Messiah; Ps 2.7] with whom I am well pleased [i.e., my Servant; Isa 42.1].' Jesus took this fundamental option to be a Servant-Messiah and thus 'became obedient unto death, even unto death on the cross' (Phil 2.8). This option was challenged not only during the temptations in the desert (Mk 1.12–13; Mt 4.1–11; Lk 4.1–13) – which, in fact are a summary of the temptations Jesus faced throughout his ministry – but on all occasions in which people tried to make Jesus change his mind concerning that fundamental option. Time and again, Peter, the scribes and the Pharisees, and those who passed under the cross, challenged him to change his mind. They tempted him to perform astonishing signs and to reach the goal of his mission by making common cause with the powers that be. But to this temptation Jesus never gave in. He continued to go his way as *Servant*-Messiah – *not*, however, as a subservient Messiah. Jesus was not at all awed by the powers of his time. When told that Herod was after him, he answered, 'Go and tell that fox . . .' (Lk 13.32). He was referring to the highest political authority in Galilee! When Pilate asked him, 'Are you the king of the Jews?' Jesus answered, 'Do you say this of your own accord, or did others say it to you about me?' (Jn 18.33–34). Thus he addressed the representative of the Roman emperor! Now, there cannot be any doubt that the Gospels, especially Matthew, were written on the basis of the premise 'Like Christ, like Church.'[50] So, the Church too should be a *Servant*-Church without at any time being a *subservient* Church. She should be a Church that is ready to take a stand wherever moral values, like justice and integrity, are set at naught – especially when this is done by those whose mandate it is to uphold these values!

> To say that we are not to take the offensive against the powers is to ignore the whole thrust of God's action in history. In the incarnation, God Himself steps into history to join battle with the forces of evil. Jesus took the offensive and constantly battled with the demonic forces during His public ministry . . . As the body of Christ, we are to continue the mission of the incarnate One in the world today and that includes an ongoing offensive against the fallen principalities and powers, a vigorous active use of power in the search for greater justice in society.[51]

Or, in the words of the Catholic Bishops of the Philippines *Pastoral Letter* of 13 February 1986:

> We are not going to effect the change we seek by doing nothing, by sheer apathy. If we did nothing, we would be party to our own destruction as a people. We would be jointly guilty with the perpetrators of the wrong we want righted . . . The way indicated to us now is the way of non-violent struggle for justice. This means active resistance of evil by peaceful means – in the manner of Christ. And its one end for now is that the will of the people be done through ways and means proper to the Gospel.

And so we reach the unavoidable question, 'What then shall we do?' (Lk 3.10). Again the gospel should be our guide. However, it is often maintained that Jesus lived in a very different time and culture. This is true, of course, but the statement should not be generalized, even less absolutized.

The German New Testament scholar, Martin Hengel, summarizes the background of violence and oppression in the Roman empi.ε of Jesus' day (so full of surprising parallels to the injustice and violence of our own time) and the repeated Jewish attempts at armed rebellion.

For the unsophisticated Jewish population, it was almost entirely a history of oppressive exploitation, wars of indescribable brutality and disappointed hopes . . . The rule of Herod and his sons and the corrupt regime of the procurators – Pilate not least among them – had made the situation in Jewish Palestine so intolerable that apparently only *three possibilities* remained: armed revolutionary resistance, more or less opportunistic accommodation of the establishment (*critical cooperation*?) – leaving open the possibility of mental reservations – and patient passive endurance.[52]

It was into this maelstrom of oppression, violence, and intense messianic expectation that Jesus of Nazareth stepped to proclaim and incarnate a *fourth possibility* – the way of suffering servanthood.

It is within this dark context, which was certainly no less desperate for the Jews in Palestine than all today's oppression in Latin America or elsewhere in the world, that Jesus' message and ministry must be 'sketched' if we are to understand it correctly today. In a radically new way he presented an alternative allowing men to escape from these *three hopeless possibilities*, to break out of the vicious circle of violence and counterviolence, opportunistic complicity, and apathetic resignation, an alternative that has not lost its significance for today.[53]

Jesus kept a *critical distance* from the political powers and authorities of his period (Mt 11.8; Lk 13.32;

22.25). For him they are emptied of power by the nearness of God; they had become, so to speak, indifferent matters (Mk 12.13–17; cf. Mt 17.25ff.). Among the followers of Jesus not their laws but the order of love and service are in force (Mk 10.42ff.; Lk 22.24ff.). Thus the individual, regardless of his situation, is 'empowered' to freedom in the face of all the powers that would oppress his humanity. He therefore passes harsh judgment upon unjust 'worldly wealth' (Lk 16.9, 11), which in his time – as still today in lands with a feudal structure – stood in brutal contrast to the poverty of the bulk of the population. With his alternative 'either God or worldly wealth' (Mt 6.24) and his requirement to put away anxious thought (Mt 6.25ff.) he strikes to the roots of human existence. But even these demands are not based on some binding 'social program' but on the offer of unconditional trust in the goodness of the Father . . . None of his contemporaries criticized more sharply than he the complacent, self-satisfied Babbitts[54] that sought the meaning of life primarily in the acquisition of riches. His message was thus socially and politically explosive . . . If it were not so, it would be almost impossible to understand why the lower classes came to him in such droves; for this very reason he aroused suspicions and fears of the national leaders, of Herod Antipas in Galilee and the Sanhedrin in Jerusalem. This appeal to the '*am ha-'ares*', the uneducated people 'who do not know the law' and are therefore accused, he may also share with the revolutionists. But he never allowed this openness to the religiously and socially déclassé, despised by the upper classes, to be restricted by political barriers. he addressed himself not only to the totally 'useless', the poorest of the poor, the sick – the lepers, for instance – but also to the 'traitors to the nation' and 'exploiters', the universally hated tax collectors . . . In other words, Jesus' message could not be pigeonholed in any of the contemporary religious or political schemata; his critical attitude touched in fundamental terms all the contemporary 'parties' in Palestine.[55]

Jürgen Moltmann has said that 'everything that can be categorized as "non-violence" in the sayings and actions of Jesus can ultimately be derived from this "revolution in the concept of God" which he set forth; namely that God comes not to carry out just revenge upon the evil, but to justify sinners by grace, whether they are Zealots or tax collectors, Pharisees or sinners.'[56]

The *ultimate* effect of Jesus' coming on earth may be reconciliation to God and enduring peace; but the *immediate* effect of this proclamation is often division and conflict. In other words, the call for *decision* may in the present often be a call for *division*. And that is where the conflict comes in. In fact, 'the cross stands as a harsh reminder that love for enemies does not always work – at least in the short run.'[57]

That is how the establishment settled their accounts with Jesus.

But even to the revolutionary Zealots Jesus appeared hardly less dangerous than to the establishment, for (1) he had great influence among the simple rural population of Galilee, in other words, their primary source of recruits; and (2) his demand for love of enemies and renunciation of violence was in extreme opposition to their ideal of revolutionary zeal. They therefore necessarily perceived his message as a direct threat. He appeared simultaneously as a 'competitor' and a 'traitor'. This means that both the extreme right and the left of Jesus' period rejected him as an intolerable provocation, and his death was undoubtedly welcomed by both wings.[58]

But we should have a closer look at the implications of the use of violence or force. We believe that the use of economic and political power may be, and indeed is, fully compatible with Jesus' way of suffering servanthood. There are many kinds of power, and correspondingly of force or violence. Force is present in every social setting. It is present in economics and politics. We reject the comforting distinction some people do draw between 'violence' as the improper use of 'force', and 'force' as 'violence sanctioned by law'. Anything that hurts people is violence. But it is possible to distinguish between forms of force or violence which love and respect the other person as a free moral agent responsible to the Creator, and forms of force and violence which do not.

We need to become co-workers with the oppressed as they rightly search for a more just distribution of power in our world. For some that will mean persistent, uncompromising advocacy of the rights of the oppressed from within present economic and political systems. For others it will mean economic boycotts, demonstrations, civil disobedience and the building of alternative institutions. For both groups, it will mean ongoing prayer and dialogue to see when conscientious objection, conscientious refusal to participate in a given corporation, election, or office is the only faithful, effective way to exercise power.'[59]

It is possible then, to use some forms of force or

'violence' in a way that respects the other person. Lethal violence is different. To kill another person is to treat him or her like a thing not a person. Hence we believe that Jesus' teaching excludes lethal violence as an acceptable option for real Christians. (But what about extreme cases? Think, for example of Dietrich Bonhoeffer, who was very serious about the Sermon on the Mount but nevertheless joined the plot against Adolf Hitler.)

The injustice and suffering in Palestine two thousand years ago was certainly no less than the suffering in our world today. The revolutionary prescriptions of our time for the overcoming of such injustice and suffering are likewise not always so very different from those proposed then. The idea that the present-day situation has become intolerable, so that revolutionary violence has become justified, even necessary, was widespread then as now – and it was not the most wicked who were proclaiming this idea. Those who justify violence which they can scarcely escape, and which – as is shown by the history of the revolutions . . . – will either corrupt them through abuse of their new-found power or, if they seek to preserve their 'humanity', drive them into opposition and finally liquidate them as alleged 'counter-revolutionaries'.[60]

Jesus was not a pacifist in *principle*, he was a pacifist *in practice*, that is to say, in the concrete circumstances of his time. We do not know what he would have done in other possible circumstances. But we can surmise that *if* there had been no other way of defending the poor and the oppressed and *if* there had been no danger of an escalation of violence, his unlimited compassion might have overflowed temporarily into a violent indignation . . . However, even in such cases, violence would be a temporary measure with no other purpose than the prevention of some more serious violence. The kingdom of total liberation for all men cannot be established by violence. Faith alone can enable the kingdom to come.[61]

Discussion Questions

1. What were the political options which Jesus faced?

2. How similar to and how different from our world today was the world of Jesus?

3. What did Jesus mean by saying 'Do not resist one who is evil'?

4. What is structural injustice?

5. Did Jesus approve or disapprove the use of violence? Try to support your answer by referring to Jesus' overall message and praxis.

6. Did Jesus categorically and absolutely reject all forms of violence?

7. Can a Christian, after having given due consideration to the gospel message, decide in conscience to get involved in a line of action which may eventually lead to the use of some forms of violence? Support your answer.

Notes

1. X. Leon-Dufour, 'Peace,' in *Dictionary of Biblical Theology* (second edition; London: Geoffrey Chapman, 1973), pp. 412–413.
2. G. von Rad, '*Eirene*,' in G. Kittel and G. Friedrich (eds.), *Theological Dictionary of the New Testament* vol. II (London: SCM Press, 1964), p. 406.
3. Ibid. pp. 402–403.
4. W. Foerster, '*Eirene*,' in *Theological Dictionary of the New Testament* vol. II, pp. 400–402.
5. C.H. Talbert, *Reading Luke: A Literary and Theological Commentary on the Third Gospel* (New York: Crossroad, 1984), p. 33.
6. M. Black, ' "Not Peace but a Sword": Matt. 10:34ff.; Luke 12:51ff.,' in E. Bammel and C.F.D. Moule (eds.), *Jesus and the Politics of His Day* (Cambridge: Cambridge University Press, 1984), p. 287.
7. J.A. Fitzmyer, *The Gospel According to Luke X-XXIV* (Anchor Bible 28A; Garden City, N.Y.: Doubleday, 1985), p. 995.
8. M. Black op. cit., pp. 289, 293–294.
9. C. Marney, *Faith in Conflict* (New York: Abingdon Press, 1957), p. 12.
10. E. Best, *The First and Second Epistles to the Thessalonians* (London: A & C Black, 1972), p. 207.
11. C.J. Peifer, 'Peace According to St Paul,' *The Bible Today* 21 (3 May 1983), pp. 174–175.
12. Ibid. p. 175.
13. F.W. Danker, *Invitation to the New Testament. Epistles IV* (Image Books; Garden City, N.Y.: Doubleday, 1980), pp. 108–109.

14. P. Davids, *The Epistle of James: A Commentary on the Greek Text* (Exeter: Paternoster Press, 1982), p. 155.

15. R.E. Brown, *The Gospel According to John*, vol. 2 (London: Geoffrey Chapman, 1971), p. 653.

16. B. Lindars, *The Gospel of John* (New Century Bible; London: Marshall, Morgan & Scott, 1981), p. 484.

17. L. Morris, *The Gospel According to John* (Grand Rapids: Eerdmans, 1971), pp. 657–658.

18. R.E. Brown, op. cit., p. 738.

19. These data are taken from N. Lohfink (ed.), *Gewalt und Gewaltlosigkeit in Alten Testament* (Quaestiones Disputatae 96; Freiburg: Herder, 1983), p. 15.

20. This chapter is based on J. Pons, *L'Oppression dans l'Ancien Testament* (Paris: Letouzey et Ané, 1981), pp. 27–52.

21. G.E. Wright, *The Old Testament and Theology* (New York: Harper and Row, 1969), pp. 122–123.

22. Ibid. pp. 130–131.

23. Cf. J.L. McKenzie, *The Old Testament Without Illusions* (Chicago: Thomas More Press, 1979), pp. 209–219.

24. J.M. Ford, *My Enemy is My Guest. Jesus and Violence in Luke* (Maryknoll, N.Y.: Orbis Books, 1984), pp. 1–3.

25. Ibid. pp. 3–12, 65–70, 79–86.

26. F.W. Danker, *Jesus and the New Age: A Commentary on the Third Gospel* (St Louis: Clayton Publishing House, 1972), p. 27.

27. Cf. D.E. Garland, *The Intention of Matthew 23* (Leiden: E.J. Brill, 1979), pp. 141–150.

28. Cf. I.H. Marshall, *The Gospel of Luke: A Commentary on the Greek Text* (Exeter: Paternoster Press, 1978), pp. 494–495.

29. Cf. J.A. Fitzmyer, op. cit., pp. 1117–1118.

30. J.D. Crossan, 'Jesus and Pacifism,' in J.W. Flanagan (ed.), *No Famine in the Land. Studies in Honor of John L. McKenzie* (Missoula: Scholars Press, 1975), pp. 196–197.

31. R.J. Sider, *Christ and Violence* (Scottdale: Herald Press, 1979), pp. 47–49.

32. J.A. Fitzmyer op. cit., p. 1029.

33. W. Grundmann, 'The Decision of the Supreme Court to Put Jesus to Death (John 11:47–57) in its Context: Tradition and Redaction in th Gospel of John,' in E. Bammel and C.F.D. Moule (eds.), *Jesus and the Politics of his Day* (Cambridge: Cambridge University Press, 1985), pp. 301–303.

34. J.C. Fenton, *The Passion According to John* (London: SPCK, 1961), p. 38.

35. E. Trocmé, *Jesus and His Contemporaries* (London: SCM Press, 1973), pp. 112–113.

36. M. Hengel, *Was Jesus a Revolutionist?* (Philadelphia: Fortress Press, 1971), pp. 16–17.

37. A. Nolan, *Jesus Before Christianity* (London: Darton, Longman and Todd, 1977), pp. 102–103. It is also interesting to note that J. Miranda, *Marx and the Bible: A Critique of the Philosophy of Oppression* (London: SCM Press, 1977) does not have a single reference to the cleansing of the temple in any of its four versions.

38. J.M. Ford, op. cit., p. 115.

39. The most extensive study I could get hold of is an unpublished thesis: N.B. Steen, *The Interpretation of Jesus' Sword-Saying in Luke 22:35—38* (Grand Rapids: Calvin Theological Seminary, 1981), vi + 135 pp. I have made extensive use of this thesis.

40. J.A. Fitzmyer, op. cit., p. 1434.

41. P.S. Minear, 'A Note on Luke 22:36,' *Novum Testamentum* 7 (1964), p. 131.

42. As quoted by M. Hengel, op. cit., p. 8.

43. Cullmann, *The State in the New Testament* (London: SCM Press, 1963) and *Jesus and the Revolutionaries* (New York: Harper and Row, 1970).

44. O. Cullmann, *The State*, p. 31.

45. O. Cullmann, *Revolutionaries*, pp. 48–49.

46. H. Conzelmann, *The Theology of St Luke* (London: Faber and Faber, 1970), p. 82.

47. Compare A. Rizzi, 'Toward an Anthropology of Peace,'

Theology Digest 32 (2, Summer 1985), p. 128.
48. A. Nolan, *Taking Sides* (London: Catholic Truth Society), pp. 1–6.
49. R.J. Sider, op. cit., pp. 46–47.
50. H. Hendricks, *One Jesus – Four Gospels* (Manila: Apostolic Center Press, 1982).
51. R.J. Sider, op. cit., pp. 57–58.
52. M. Hengel, *Victory Over Violence* (London: SPCK, 1975), p. 71.
53. Ibid. pp. 71–72.
54. 'Babbitt' is a person who conforms to prevailing middle-class standards of respectability, esteems material success, and is contemptuous of artistic and intellectual values.
55. M. Hengel, op. cit., pp. 76–79.
56. J. Moltmann, *The Crucified God* (London: SCM Press, 1976), p. 142.
57. R.J. Sider, op. cit., p. 28.
58. M. Hengel, op. cit., p. 80.
59. R.J. Sider, op. cit., p. 62.
60. M. Hengel, op. cit., pp. 83–84.
61. A. Nolan, *Jesus Before Christianity*, p. 111.

IMAGING THE GOSPELS
Kathy Galloway

'Kathy Galloway's imaginative meditations bring familiar gospel passages alive in a way that many people will find exciting and liberating. They will be particularly helpful for those who are unfamiliar with the use of the imagination in prayer and biblical meditation.'

Charles Elliott

'Her book is full of striking and useful insights. It invites us to meet the Jesus of the Gospels, who challenges, strengthens and gives us hope today.'

Gerard Hughes

AGENDA FOR BIBLICAL PEOPLE
Jim Wallis

This thought-provoking book sets out a spiritual and practical strategy for people who wish to be fully biblical in the personal, political and economic areas of their lives.

FORGIVE AND FORGET
Healing the hurts we don't deserve
Lewis Smedes

We may forgive the personal wrongs done to us; but do we have the right to forgive wrongs done to others – like violence to a child or, on an international scale, the horrors of the holocaust? Lewis Smedes comes to grips with these hard questions and takes us through the four stages of forgiveness – hurt, hate, healing and reconciliation – which can heal deep-seated pain stemming from even harsh and undeserved wrongs which we have suffered. He also addresses the hardest question of all: When you have no one to blame, can you forgive God?

All titles are available from bookshops, or from the Mail Order Department, SPCK, Holy Trinity Church, Marylebone Road, London NW1 4DU. Tel 01–387–5282. Please write or telephone for details of prices and postage, and ask for your free copy of the SPCK complete catalogue.